PRAYERS OF THE PEOPLE

PRAYERS OF THE PEOPLE

Petitionary Prayers Guided by the Texts for the Day

Richard F. Bansemer

ALPB BOOKS

DELHI, NEW YORK

The American Lutheran Publicity Bureau wishes to acknowledge with deep appreciation John Hannah for proofreading the prayers when they were originally published on the Lutheran Forum website, William Fensterer for proofreading the text, and Dorothy Zelenko for copyediting, typesetting, design and production.
Frederick J. Schumacher
Executive Director, ALPB

Copyright ©2014
American Lutheran Publicity Bureau
All rights reserved in the United States of America

The citations of the texts for each day and the assigned calendar dates for Sundays after Pentecost are from the *Revised Common Lec*tionary copyright © 1992 Consultation on Common Texts, admin. Augsburg Fortress. Reproduced by permission of Augsburg Fortress.

American Lutheran Publicity Bureau
P.O. Box 327
Delhi, New York 13753

ISBN 1-892921-25-1

Richard F. Bansemer, *Prayers of the People: Petitionary Prayers Guided by the Texts for the Day*
Delhi, NY: ALPB Books, 2014

Contents

Introduction xx
Advent, Year A 1
Christmas, Year A 5
Epiphany 9
Sundays after Epiphany, Year A 10
The Transfiguration, Year A 18
Ash Wednesday 19
Sundays in Lent, Year A 20
Sunday of the Passion, Palm Sunday, Year A 25
Maundy Thursday 26
Good Friday 27
Easter Season, Year A 28
The Day of Pentecost, Year A 35
The Holy Trinity, Year A 36
Time after Pentecost, Year A 37
Reformation Sunday 60
All Saints Sunday, Year A 61
Christ the King, Year A 65
Advent, Year B 67
Christmas, Year B 71
Epiphany 75
Sundays after Epiphany, Year B 76
The Transfiguration, Year B 84
Ash Wednesday 85

Sundays in Lent, Year B	86
Sunday of the Passion, Palm Sunday, Year B	91
Maundy Thursday	92
Good Friday	93
Easter Season, Year B	94
The Day of Pentecost, Year B	101
The Holy Trinity, Year B	102
Time after Pentecost, Year B	103
Reformation Sunday	126
All Saints Sunday, Year B	127
Christ the King, Year B	131
Advent, Year C	133
Christmas, Year C	137
Epiphany	141
Sundays after Epiphany, Year C	142
The Transfiguration, Year C	150
Ash Wednesday	151
Sundays in Lent, Year C	152
Sunday of the Passion, Palm Sunday, Year C	157
Maundy Thursday	158
Good Friday	159
Easter Season, Year C	160
The Day of Pentecost, Year C	167
The Holy Trinity, Year C	168
Time after Pentecost, Year C	169
Reformation Sunday	192
All Saints Sunday, Year C	193
Christ the King, Year C	197

Introduction

About the Prayers

These Prayers of the Church seek to incorporate the lessons of the day in petitions to God. With some latitude, the form usually begins with a reflective prayer on the Old Testament, then the Psalm of the day, the Epistle lesson, and finally the Gospel. Sometimes a lesson may have more than one petition, and sometimes a petition may include an alternate lesson for the day.

The idea is to bring before God what has been said to us in Holy Scripture, in a way that expresses hope, thanksgiving, admiration, struggle and joy. Most every prayer will name God as Father, Son and Holy Spirit somewhere among the petitions.

Every prayer also includes a petition for healing. Additional petitions for the concerns of the day, the world, and the local community may be added. The congregational response may be altered, along with the petitions themselves, to meet the needs of the pastor or liturgist in public prayer before the congregation.

About the Lectionary

The texts to which the prayers relate are those in the Revised Common Lectionary (RCL) published in 1992 by the Consultation on Common Texts and now in use by many Christian churches, including most Lutherans, in the United States and Canada. The prayers in this book are arranged by year—A, B and C—and season. The scriptural citations from the RCL appear at the bottom of each prayer. For the prayers for the Sundays after Pentecost, the calendar date range when those lessons are used are also given.

The number of Sundays after Epiphany and after Pentecost varies from year to year, depending on the day of the week of Christmas Day and the calendar date of Easter. In the case of Sundays after Epiphany, Lutherans observe them in order until the Sunday before Ash Wednesday when they skip those for any remaining Sundays after Epiphany and go ahead to observe the Sunday of the Transfiguration on that day.

In the case of Sundays after Pentecost, The Holy Trinity is always observed on the First Sunday after Pentecost. On the Second Sunday after Pentecost, one moves forward to whichever Lectionary number is assigned for that Sunday's calendar date.

The effect of these guides is that the readings for the Sundays after the Epiphany that are not used in some years are those at the end of the cycle, while the readings omitted from the Sundays after Pentecost are those at the beginning of the cycle. This way of assigning the readings after Pentecost means that a certain set of texts is consistently related to a calendar date range rather than to, for example, the 10th Sunday after Pentecost. For this reason the prayers for the Sundays after Pentecost in this book are identified by their Lectionary numbers and date ranges.

A Note of Personal Thanks

Thank you, Dorothy Zelenko, for using your skills, tireless devotion, theological acumen and sense of churchmanship as reflected in the way this book is organized, edited and presented as a tool for worship. I am sincerely grateful.

Richard F. Bansemer

1st Sunday of Advent

Responsive Sentence for Advent:
    Stir up your power and come: **Be born anew in us.**

Heavenly Father, we enter this new church year with song, wreath and lessons. The very coming of our Lord and Savior Jesus Christ is near. Stir up in us a yearning heart, an open mind, a spirit seeking your Spirit as company for our journey of faith. And when the day of birth for Jesus finally comes, may He be born in each of us also. **R**

Lord Jesus Christ, you have come and are coming. You have been here from the beginning, you have been here in time, and now you come to us in this very hour. You remind us about yet another day, and another hour, another coming of which no one knows the moment, except the Father. You bid us to be ready. **R**

We bring before you, Holy Spirit, all the other spirits that would rob us of the joy of Jesus' coming. We fearfully invite you to help us rid ourselves of all the temporal and earthly concerns of this season, so that we may truly focus upon God incarnate, God in flesh, God for real, God with us now. **R**

Known to us, Lord, are persons with needs beyond our own ability to fix. We thank you for all who attend to the sick, the weary, and the ones who feel separated from you, the church, even each other. Hear our prayers for those whom we name who need a special measure of your grace: _____. As you come to them and be their healer, hear us pray. **R**

In a world of rich resources, help us remember the poor, not only in memory, but also in love, for they are our brothers and sisters. Use our caring, giving, helping, and living with the poor as ways to be your incarnation. And may we see you incarnate in them. **R**

We yearn, Father, for the day when nations shall beat their swords into plowshares. We yearn for the day of peace, when we can all walk in the gentle light of Christ. We look to your Son, who lived another way, taught a different lesson, emanated the Holy Spirit, and died a sacrificial death. He is the Messiah, and through Him we boldly pray. **R**

All the earth, seas, and heavens are yours, and we pray these prayers because you have promised to listen to us. **Amen.**

Texts: Isaiah 2:1-5,   Psalm 122,   Romans 13:11-14,   Matthew 24:36-44

YEAR A

2nd Sunday of Advent

Responsive Sentence for Advent:
    Stir up your power and come: **Be born anew in us.**

We know, Heavenly Father, that the words of John the Baptist, "Repent, for the kingdom of heaven has come near," were meant for all ages, all peoples, for all of us. We confess we hardly know how to repent. Beginning again, turning around, admitting wrong . . . not easy for us. Yet you send us this messenger whose primary word is "Repent." Open our eyes as well as our ears, our hearts as well as our minds, so we may understand the necessity of being born anew. **R**

We see the vision of Isaiah's new world when the earth will be full of the knowledge of your Messiah Son. The wolf and the lamb, the bear and the cow, the child and the asp will be at peace. Give us a vision too, that we may believe with the Psalmist that love and faithfulness will meet, and that righteousness and peace will kiss each other. **R**

Holy Spirit, fill us with expectation, like you did Paul, whom you filled with hope. Keep us from latching onto wishful thinking. Instead, turn us to true hope, with the full expectation of your presence in our every moment of our every day, now and forever. **R**

You are a God of justice, dear Father. Help us understand your judgments. We see you loving the poor, those who languish, and the oppressed. You promise that peace will abound, and that righteousness will flourish. Give us the eye of Christ to see it. **R**

With joy and thanksgiving we come to your table of presence, Lord Jesus, knowing that we have been blessed beyond measure. You love us, accept us, visit us as children from mangers, born with nothing, but now your precious children. **R**

Finally, we pray for those whom you have placed into our lives and into our care. We name before you those with special need: _____. Great Physician, we know that you are already bearing their burdens, healing their diseases, along with those of the multitude of others you alone know by name. **R**

All the earth, seas, and heavens are yours, and we pray these prayers because you have promised to listen to us. **Amen**.

Texts: Isaiah 11:1-10   Psalm 72:1-7, 18-19   Romans 15:4-13   Matthew 3:1-12

YEAR A

3rd Sunday of Advent

Responsive Sentence for Advent:
    Stir up your power and come: **Be born anew in us.**

Lord Jesus Christ, like John the Baptist we want to know if you are the Messiah. You tell us to listen and to take notice of you in this world, and then, from experience, you talk about the kingdom of heaven. Open our eyes to see the lame walking, cures occurring, and hope rising in the kingdom that shall come, all as evidence of your presence among us. **R**

Dearest Father, your glory is made manifest by the strength you give us as your believing people. Fear dissipates when you are near. Weak knees no longer tremble. We want to sing, and joy replaces doubt. We reach for you with our feeble hands, but it's your hand that holds us fast. **R**

Holy Spirit, we need your counsel. We do not wait well. Like farmers waiting for crops to ripen, we need to remember that your time and presence saturates all of our days, especially those in which nothing much seems to be happening. And then you make us bloom in due season. **R**

We remember, Lord, that you set the prisoners free, and gave justice to the wronged. Now you care for parent-less children and surviving spouses through us, your hands and heart and voice in a world that does not see loneliness as suffering. Be present through us as we attend to all in need. **R**

As we name those whom we know have special needs for healing, remind us of our own need to be prayed for by the faithful. Hear us as we speak aloud, or in our hearts, the names of those who need you, even as we whisper our very own names: _____. **R**

Soon, Jesus, comes the Day of Christmas, your incarnation. Help us, like children, to feel the excitement, for we are all children of the Heavenly Father. **R**

All the earth, seas, and heavens are yours, and we pray these prayers because you have promised to listen to us. **Amen**.

Texts: Isaiah 35:1-10   Psalm 146:5-10 or Luke 1:46b-55   James 5:7-10   Matthew 11:2-11

YEAR A

4th Sunday of Advent

Responsive Sentence for Advent:
    Stir up your power and come: **Be born anew in us.**

With the Psalmist, Heavenly Father, we dare pray "Stir up your might." We even ask to be restored. We want to see your face shine, that we may know that you are our God, and we are your people. The celebration of your Son's birth on earth is near. **R**

Holy Spirit, even as Paul was set apart for the gospel of God, you call us also to be your saints. As we proclaim the good news of the resurrection from the dead, remind us that we belong to your Son, Jesus Christ. **R**

Lord Jesus, Son of God, you became a human being. Stepping down from heaven's glory, you put on our flesh. No person can match what you have given. We are eternally grateful, and we ask you to help us imitate you in our thinking, in our speaking, and through our deeds. **R**

The fulfillment of the expectation of this season is upon us, and there will be joy as we remember the struggle of Joseph, the pain of Mary, and the counsel you give us: "Do not be afraid." **R**

We remember the sick, the weary, and especially the lonely this season. Help us say Emmanuel, God is with us, by our care, our cards, our gifts and our reunions. Listen as we name those names you already know, but which we need to speak: _____. **R**

All the earth, seas, and heavens are yours, and we pray these prayers because you have promised to listen to us. **Amen.**

Texts: Isaiah 7:10-16   Psalm 80:1-7, 17-19   Romans 1:1-7   Matthew 1:18-25

Nativity of Our Lord
Christmas Eve, December 24th

Responsive Sentence for Christmas Eve:
    Do not be afraid: **The news is good.**

Isaiah is singing, Lord God, and his joy is overwhelming. The great light shines on all who have walked in darkness. You break all oppressors' rods, even our own yokes to sin. You come to us as a child this night. You are the Wonderful Counselor, the Mighty God, the Everlasting Father, the Prince of Peace. **R**

We sing a new song with the Psalmist, Lord God, thanking you for your salvation, your glory, your marvelous work that makes the heavens glad and the earth rejoice. You are our king! You shall never be moved. You judge us fairly, knowing our humanness, and you judge us with truth and with righteousness. **R**

Lord Jesus, though there was no room for you in the inn, you were born anyway. Come to the mangers of our individual lives, the rudest places of our need, and be born in us again, that we might be born again in you. **R**

Like Mary and Joseph and the shepherds in the field, we have heard the angel's counsel: "Do not be afraid." Help us not be afraid as strange and wondrous gifts of your love come also to us. **R**

May our singing join with the voices of the shepherds and angels, giving witness and making song: "Glory to God in the highest, and peace to his people on earth." **Amen.**

Texts: Isaiah 9:2-7   Psalm 96   Titus 2:11-14   Luke 2:1-14 [15-20]

YEAR A

Nativity of Our Lord
Christmas Day, December 25th

Responsive Sentence for Christmas Day:
    The Lord has comforted his people: **Our God reigns.**

The messenger on the mountain, Lord Father, has beautiful feet because he brings us good news of your Son, your Word incarnate, your Word made flesh. The sentinels shout in joy, for in plain sight you return to Zion. Open our eyes to see, our ears to hear, your incarnate Word, Jesus Christ. **R**

Long ago, Heavenly Father, you came to us through prophets, priests and kings, but now you come to us through your Son, your only Son, Jesus Christ. He is your imprint. He is your heir. He was with you when you created the world. He reflects your glory. He is superior to all angels. You have anointed Him with the oil of gladness. **R**

In the beginning was the Word. Perhaps it was a soft word. Perhaps it was a whispered word. Maybe you shouted! Whatever it was, you broke the silence of all eons. You filled space with material stuff. You created all there is out of nothing, just by speaking your Word. All that we use our senses to see, taste, touch, smell and hear came from your voice, and it is good. **R**

In the beginning, your Son was with you . . . present at the creation. In Him was life, and that life is the light of all people. Though the world came into being through Him, the world did not, does not, recognize Him. Yet his glory is full of grace and truth. Those who receive Him become the children of God, the highest calling on earth. **R**

We give you thanks for this birthday that is above every birthday, for you came to live among us, as one of us, and to accomplish all things for our salvation. **Amen.**

Texts: Isaiah 62:6-12   Psalm 97   Titus 3:4-7   Luke 2:[1-7] 8-20

1st Sunday after Christmas Day

Responsive Sentence for 1st Sunday after Christmas Day:
 Young men and women, old and young together: **Praise the LORD!**

LORD God, out of love and mercy you have sent us your best. Jesus is your very presence, your only Son, as the babe in the manger, as the Lord of our lives. **R**

All the heavens, all angels, sun, moon and shining stars praise you, LORD. The earth and her seas and all living things praise you. **R**

All things exist because of you, Heavenly Father. All the redeemed have one Father, and Jesus is therefore proud to call us brothers and sisters. **R**

Lord Jesus Christ, sharing with us a flesh and blood body, you identify with us like no other. You alone are able to free us from the fear of death, because you came to destroy the devil who has the power of death. You suffered for us. You were tested and made a sacrifice of atonement for the sins of all people. **R**

Lord Holy Spirit, help us see the flight to Egypt as God's protection in real lives, in real time, and in historical fact. Your way is not a figment of imagination, not a dreamy ideal of a better time, but a true, actual, living event in history. Help us see your work in our earthly lives. **R**

We thank you for the faith of Mary and Joseph. Like them, we ask you to give us the courage to hear your word and to do your bidding in all things. In our wanderings and in our sufferings may we remember you are LORD. For those who, for a time, have been sent to a foreign place, and for those with special needs, hear our prayers for restoration to family, friends and health: _____. **R**
Amen.

Texts: Isaiah 63:7-9;   Psalm 148,   Hebrews 2:10-18,   Matthew 2:13-23

YEAR A

2nd Sunday after Christmas Day

Responsive Sentence for 2nd Sunday after Christmas Day:
  Once born in Bethlehem: **Be born in us today.**

Almighty God, you comfort us and turn our mourning into joy when you guide us back into your presence. Help us "be radiant with the goodness of the LORD." **R**

Holy Spirit, bless our children, grant us peace, give favorable weather and water to all, and help us love your most holy word. **R**

Heavenly Father, you chose us before the foundation of the world to be blessed in Christ with the spirituality of love. As you have adopted us, help us revel in your care, your gifts, your holy will, and your plan for our eternal inheritance. **R**

Lord Jesus Christ, so close to the Heavenly Father's heart, give us the gift to believe that you have made us "children of God." **R**

Be born anew in us, Lord Jesus, that your Holy Spirit may be as real to us as our own breath, our own beating heart, our own sense of the Divine. **R**

We remember to bring before you all the saints who suffer for the faith, and all in any sort of need. Hear us as we recall them by name: _____. **R**

Let your light shine upon us and we shall be saved. **Amen.**

Texts: Jeremiah 31:7-14 or Sirach 24:1-12   Psalm 147:12-20 or Wisdom of Solomon 10:15-21   Ephesians 1:3-14
John 1:[1-9] 10-18

The Epiphany of Our Lord
January 6th

Responsive Sentence for the Epiphany of Our Lord:
   Arise, shine, for the light has come: **The glory of the LORD has risen upon us.**

Heavenly Father, through your prophet Isaiah you have promised a great light that will draw all the nations to you. Help us see your presence in our time that we may radiate your joy in our own lives. **R**

Lord Jesus Christ, you defend the cause of the poor, and deliver the needy and those who have no helper. Use us as your heart, hands and feet to care for our poorer sisters and brothers, whose lives are as precious to you as our own. You make us see all your children as our own kin. **R**

We thank you, Lord Jesus Christ, for Paul, a prisoner for your sake. From him we learn that we are fellow heirs of the mystery, and members of the same body, sharing in you the promise of the gospel's great news. Make us servants of your grace, that your boundless riches may be known to all. **R**

Lord Jesus, born in Bethlehem, you were visited by star-following wise men from the East who wanted to see you face to face. Give us this same desire to see you, for you alone are due our homage. **R**

Holy Spirit, guide us like you guided the wise men from the East. When we come into the presence of the Lord, fill us with generosity to give gifts worthy of God's great mystery revealed through Him. **R**

We remember all who have special needs—the poor, the lonely, the distraught, those who sense no love, and those who need your healing presence. Hear us as we name them in our hearts or aloud: _____ . **R**

Make all our petitions selfless, like those you taught us to pray. **Amen.**

Texts: Isaiah 60:1-6   Psalm 72:1-7, 10-14   Ephesians 3:1-12   Matthew 2:1-12

YEAR A

Baptism of Our Lord
1st Sunday after Epiphany

Responsive Sentence for the Sundays after Epiphany:
    Let us walk: **In the light of the Lord.**

Lord God, Creator of the universe and more, your soul delights in your chosen one, Jesus, and your Spirit is upon Him. He calls us all, takes each of us by the hand, reminds us of your holy promises, and is our Light. **R**

Glory and strength are in your voice. You have power over the flood, over the thunder of every storm, over the tree-downing wind, over every raging fire. In your gentle majesty you give strength to your people, and bless us with peace. **R**

Jesus Christ, Lord of all, anointed with the Holy Spirit and with power, you healed the sick, foiled the devil, and died hanging on the cross so that we might see that death has no more power than any other storm. You rose from the dead. You ate and drank with the disciples after your death. You are ordained by God as judge of the living and the dead. **R**

Give us the will, Holy Spirit, like John the Baptist, to do holy things for Jesus, despite our own needs. Give us the ear to hear the voice from heaven, saying to Jesus, "This is my Son, the Beloved, with whom I am well pleased." **R**

In this world filled with strife, take our hand. In this world at war, bring peace through us. In the din of too much noise, calm us with your gentle majesty, that we may serve confidently in your promises that you will fulfill all righteousness. Hear our prayers for those people with special needs, known fully by you alone, whom we name in tender thoughts and spoken words _____. **R**

Make all our petitions selfless, like those you taught us to pray. **Amen.**

Texts: Isaiah 42:1-9   Psalm 29   Acts 10:34-43   Matthew 3:13-17

2nd Sunday after Epiphany

Responsive Sentence for the Sundays after Epiphany:
    Let us walk: **In the light of the Lord.**

You command us, Heavenly Father, through your prophet Isaiah to listen and pay attention, for we are far away from you. The sharp tongues of the prophets do not let us have a glib faith. Your Son, our Savior, has been sent as our light in a dark world. **R**

Father God, you listen to us like you listened to the Psalmists when we sing our songs, cry our laments, and put our trust in your gracious mercy. Help us delight in your will. Put your law and your help in our hearts, that we may rejoice in your steadfast love. **R**

We thank you, Lord Jesus Christ, that you have called us to be saints together. As we grow in our faith in your Body, the church, fill us with your spiritual gifts, that we may not be lacking in zeal or courage. **R**

Lamb of God, John the Baptist proclaimed that you take away the sin of the world. Take away our sin, our selfishness, that we may be your people in a world that needs you more than it can admit. Help us take no offense in the fact that we need you too. **R**

Open our ears, Holy Spirit, that we may hear your call through the Scriptures, the preaching of your word, the singing of your inspired hymns, and the praying of our prayers. When we hear you call, may we walk with you as readily as Andrew and Peter. **R**

We bring before you those whom we know need healing, hope, and heavenly help. As we name them in our hearts or aloud, touch them, and us with your presence: _____. **R**

Make all our petitions selfless, like those you taught us to pray. **Amen.**

Texts: Isaiah 49:1-7   Psalm 40:1-11   1 Corinthians 1:1-9   John 1:29-42

YEAR A

3rd Sunday after Epiphany

Responsive Sentence for the Sundays after Epiphany:
    Let us walk: **In the light of the Lord.**

Heavenly Father, involved in our history from the beginning, we ask you to shine your great light upon our country, along with all other countries, whether they be friend or foe. All of us need oppression to end, darkness to vanish, and peace to reign. **R**

Lord Jesus Christ, we have no fear when you are our light and our salvation. To be a believer, to live in your house, is to behold your beauty. We sing for joy as we seek your face. **R**

Lord Jesus Christ, God incarnate, forbid us from trying to empty your cross of its power by using false wisdom or glib praise. Help us see that your cross, which is foolishness to so many, is the very power of God. **R**

Holy Spirit, as you guided the disciples to leave their nets by the sea in order to follow Jesus, inspire us to lay aside those things that are peripheral to faith. Help us see our need to repent, as both John the Baptist and Jesus preached. **R**

Great Physician, Jesus Christ, you proclaimed good news and cured all sorts of diseases among the people. We, like them, yearn for the healing of our bodies and souls. We name those whom we know who need your good news and your healing touch :_____. **R**

As the days continue to lengthen, nights shorten, and you prepare the earth for the season of spring, prepare our hearts too, that we may always walk with you. **R**

Make all our petitions selfless, like those you taught us to pray. **Amen.**

Texts: Isaiah 9:1-4   Psalm 27:1, 4-9   1 Corinthians 1:10-18   Matthew 4:12-23

4th Sunday after Epiphany

Responsive Sentence for the Sundays after Epiphany:
   Let us walk: **In the light of the Lord.**

Heavenly Father, your expectations of us are very clear. You only ask us to do justice, to love kindness and to walk humbly with you. **R**

Lord God, you live among us and expect us all to note your presence in our everyday relationships with one another. As we walk the walk of faith together, may we walk as good neighbors, doing what is right, and protecting one another from harm, injustice or unnecessary need. **R**

Lord Jesus Christ, your cross is the very power of God. It is your wisdom. It is your gift, and it is often our stumbling block. Your foolishness is wiser than our wisdom, your weakness is stronger than our strength, and you have chosen the way of the cross so that none of us may boast in your presence, unless we boast of your magnificent love for us all. **R**

Your teachings from the mountain, Lord Jesus Christ, thwart all our rationalizations for being anything other than humble and kind. May we become your blessed ones by the power of your Holy Spirit, without whose power none of us are able to do your will. **R**

We bring before you our very selves, for we are often poor in spirit, mourning, meek, hungry and thirsty for your mercy, wanting to be your child more than any other thing. Despite our failures, fill us with courage to know that when joy comes, it is your gift to us. **R**

We pray for healing for those with special needs, all known to you, since no small detail of our lives is too small for you to notice. Touch us all with your presence, and hear the names we name before you: _____. **R**

Make all our petitions selfless, like those you taught us to pray. **Amen.**

Texts: Micah 6:1-8   Psalm 15   1 Corinthians 1:18-31   Matthew 5:1-12

YEAR A

5th Sunday after Epiphany

Responsive Sentence for the Sundays after Epiphany:
Let us walk: **In the light of the Lord.**

Lord God, hearer of our every prayer, by your Holy Spirit deepen our quest to know you better and love you more deeply by caring for our sisters and brothers more ardently. Then when we call, you will answer, Here I am. **R**

Help us delight in the beauty of your commandments. When we are careful with doing what is right, we shall find joy in being gracious and merciful to others. Steady our hearts so we will never be afraid of evil tidings, but know the happiness of those who fear the LORD. **R**

As Paul sought to know nothing but Jesus Christ and Him crucified, lead us O Lord to this highest of all wisdoms. Words of eloquence are far inferior to the voice of your Holy Spirit which reveals what has been secret and hidden for the ages. May that same Spirit bring us to an understanding of the gifts given to us by God. **R**

Holy Spirit, if we are to be the salt of the earth, we must see Jesus as the light of the world. And when we see Him in our lives, may we shine with His radiance. **R**

We wish to be wise, Lord God, not with the limited wisdom of the world, but with the presence of you, Father, Son and Holy Spirit in our every moment of our every day. **R**

Remind us of the multitude of cares and concerns that are all known unto you. We remember those known to us who have special needs: _____. **R**

Make all our petitions selfless, like those you taught us to pray. **Amen.**

Texts: Isaiah 58:1-9a [9b-12]   Psalm 112:1-9 [10]   1 Corinthians 2:1-12 [13-16]   Matthew 5:13-20

6th Sunday after Epiphany

Responsive Sentence for the Sundays after Epiphany:
 Let us walk: **In the light of the Lord.**

Lord God you set before us commandments that affect our very lives. We can only obey you by loving you above all others. Give us the will and the skill to love you with all of our hearts, minds and strength. **R**

Lord Jesus, we know we are too often mere infants in the faith. We argue over big things and little things, and justify our points of view as faith. Forgive us when we do this and fail to remember that our growth in the faith is a matter of being your servant, working together with all other servants, in this world which is your mission field. **R**

Holy Spirit, help us understand the hard teachings of Jesus about anger, name-calling, bearing false witness, fidelity and marriage. Even before we come to understand, give us the strength to obey. **R**

We bring before you the needs of all countries and communities who seek to care for one another. Help us to not merely rely upon governments for justice, but to seek and do justice in our own daily lives. **R**

We look forward to the coming of spring and the flowering of the earth from her winter's sleep. Renew us also, that we may bloom like flowers, ready to bring beauty to one another. **R**

For those among us who need care, help us be the caregivers. When we name their names before you in prayer, help us also to be a real presence to those we know: _____. **R**

Make all our petitions selfless, like those you taught us to pray. **Amen.**

Texts: Deuteronomy 30:15-20 or Sirach 15:15-20   Psalm 119:1-8   1 Corinthians 3:1-9   Matthew 5:21-37

YEAR A

7th Sunday after Epiphany

Responsive Sentence for the Sundays after Epiphany:
  Let us walk: **In the light of the Lord.**

Lord God, you are very specific when you teach us to love our neighbors as ourselves. You remind us that you are our God, and that you are to be respected above all others. You call for mercy and justice from us to others, and you make all of us responsible for our judgments. Give us grace to be careful in all we say and do. **R**

You have taught us your ways, and we ask with the Psalmist to observe all that we have learned to the end of our earthly lives. Help us delight in your commandments. **R**

Lord Jesus, you have given us the task of building up the faith among all peoples. With you as our foundation, make us master builders. **R**

Holy Spirit, Counselor, help us love our enemies as Jesus taught us to do. We want to be children of the Heavenly Father. Make our judgments of one another different from the rest of the world, that we may be true to the teachings of Christ. **R**

Enter into our hearts like you enter into the innocent hearts of children, that we may be filled with joy in believing. **R**

In this world of sorrow and strife, use us to relieve the sufferings of those you put in our lives to love. Stretch our love to those beyond our own immediate family, as we name those who need your special attention: _____. **R**

Make all our petitions selfless, like those you taught us to pray. **Amen.**

Texts: Leviticus 19:1-2, 9-18   Psalm 119:33-40   1 Corinthians 3:10-11, 16-23   Matthew 5:38-48

8th Sunday after Epiphany

Responsive Sentence for the Sundays after Epiphany:
    Let us walk: **In the light of the Lord.**

Heavenly Father, you have given us your promise of comfort and great joy. Help us share your promise with the whole world. **R**

Though all the world may forget or neglect your love, Lord, forbid us from doing the same. Like a loving nursing mother you never forget us. **R**

Quiet and calm our souls, Father God, like no earthly parent can do, for even in very old age we need to know we are your children. **R**

As your servants, Lord Jesus Christ, and as stewards of God's mysteries, make us trustworthy, and keep us from making harsh judgments about one another. You alone know the purposes of every heart, even our own, and you will bring all to light when you come again. **R**

You teach us to be loyal, Holy Spirit, to the God who is God, because we cannot serve two masters. Remove worry from our hearts over food, clothing, shelter and security, for we are yours. Help us strive first for the kingdom of God. **R**

Before you are the hosts of heaven filled with angels and archangels, all bidding to do your will. Include us in this multitude of helpers as we pray for those with special needs by name: _____. **R**

Make all our petitions selfless, like those you taught us to pray. **Amen.**

Texts: Isaiah 49:8-16a   Psalm 131   1 Corinthians 4:1-5   Matthew 6:24-34

YEAR A

Transfiguration of Our Lord

Responsive Sentence for the Transfiguration of Our Lord:
    Lord of the Transfiguration: **Change us by your Word.**

Lord God, like fire on the top of Mt. Sinai, your appearance to Moses in the cloud was powerful. Now you are more likely to come to us like a babe in a manger, ready to transfigure our lives forever. **R**

Heavenly Father, in the imagination of the Psalmist, you are visualized as seated upon a throne in heaven laughing at those who counsel against you. Help us serve you in the full knowledge that you break all weapons like potter's vessels, and that we are to take refuge in you alone. **R**

Holy Spirit, you help us see the light of our Lord Jesus Christ shining like a lamp in a dark place. Help us wait for the dawn of his coming, on the last day, when all will be changed in a moment, in the twinkling of an eye. **R**

Help us read Scripture as your word, for holy men and women moved by the Holy Spirit spoke from God. **R**

Lord Jesus, on the mountain you were transfigured before Peter, James and John. You spoke with Elijah who was taken into the heavens by a chariot. You spoke with Moses, who is finally across the Jordan River. As you touched the fearful disciples and made them unafraid, touch us with the power of your presence. **R**

We look forward, Father, Son and Holy Spirit, to the day of resurrection when all will rise from the dead to meet you face to face. Give us confidence to greet you in love. Bless and heal those whom we name before you: _____. **R**
Amen.

Texts: Exodus 24:12-18   Psalm 2   2 Peter 1:16-21   Matthew 17:1-9

YEAR A

Ash Wednesday

Responsive Sentence for Ash Wednesday:
   The day of the Lord is coming: **He abounds in steadfast love.**

Lord God Almighty, your prophets warn us to tremble at your coming, for it will be a day of darkness and gloom. They advise us to return to you with our hearts, so that our gloom may be turned into the noonday sun, for you are also gracious and merciful. **R**

Have mercy on us, O God, and blot out our sins. Against you and you alone have we sinned, for all our wrong against others is against a beloved child of your own. Create in us new hearts, and put a new and right spirit within us. **R**

Lord Jesus Christ, as fellow servants of God we may be treated as imposters, yet you make us true. We may be accused of being sorrowful, but we rejoice in your presence. We may be pitied because we are seen as poor and having nothing but faith, but you make us rich in the love of God. **R**

Holy Spirit, help us hear the words of Jesus as the Word of God. Help our hearts treasure your presence more than the treasures of the world. When we do find ourselves loving you above all else, help us to be humble in spirit, for it is your gift, not our accomplishment. **R**

We bring before you those who are well aware of their physical weaknesses, for they stand in need of your healing. As we name them aloud or silently in our hearts, help us to trust you with all whom we love: _____. **R**

Though we remember we are dust and to dust we shall return, we remember that we are your precious dust. **Amen.**

Texts: Joel 2:1-2, 12-17 or Isaiah 58:1-12   Psalm 51:1-17   2 Corinthians 5:20b—6:10   Matthew 6:1-6, 16-21

YEAR A

1st Sunday in Lent

Responsive Sentence for the Sundays in Lent:
  The day of the Lord is coming: **He abounds in steadfast love.**

Heavenly Father, like Adam and Eve we often listen to the wrong voice, turning away from your Word. We are shamed by our disobedience, our deafness, our limited ability to do the right thing at the right time, or even sometimes to know what is the right thing and the right time. Forgive us, Lord, for we are weak. **R**

Hear our confession, Lord Jesus Christ, for we can hide nothing from you. Holding on to our sin only multiplies our sin, so help us say to you what we can barely admit to ourselves: we are sorry for our wrongs. **R**

Holy Spirit, we do not like to talk about sin, for it is all too personal. Governments, leaders, persons of all persuasions seek to justify themselves in all they do and say. We join with them when we refuse to come before our Lord Jesus Christ, standing in the need of forgiveness. **R**

Lord Jesus, you taught us to pray to Our Father, "Lead us not into temptation." As you were tempted in the wilderness and used the mighty Word of God to prevail against your tempter, help us do the same, that the evil one may have no power over us. **R**

As the season of spring nears, help us sense the miracle of the seed, the sun, the earth, the water. Warm our hearts, water our spirits with the memory of our baptisms, and help us grow in grace, that we may produce fruit for you. **R**

For those known to us with special needs, hear us as we name them aloud or silently, believing that all healing is a gift from you: _____. **R**

Though we remember we are dust and to dust we shall return, we remember that we are your precious dust. **Amen.**

Texts: Genesis 2:15-17; 3:1-7   Psalm 32   Romans 5:12-19   Matthew 4:1-11

2nd Sunday in Lent

Responsive Sentence for the Sundays in Lent:
   The day of the Lord is coming: **He abounds in steadfast love.**

Heavenly Father, as you sent Abraham out to a new place and a new land, so you invite us to anticipate worlds and realms beyond our imaginations. As we journey in faith, bless us with your presence that our new life in your new world may be as real as this day we call "today." **R**

Holy Spirit, our heavenly helper, you call us to worship the LORD, our keeper. He does not slumber nor sleep. He preserves our lives forevermore. **R**

Lord Jesus Christ, life-giver to the dead, with the Father and the Holy Spirit you call into existence things that do not exist, things too wonderful for us to even imagine. You justify the ungodly with your own righteousness, and by faith we receive your grace as a pure gift. **R**

Lord Jesus, as you taught Nicodemus heavenly things, give us ears to hear your Heavenly Word, and a heart to accept your grace of a new birth from above. As you were lifted up upon the cross for us, so lift our hearts in faith that we may have eternal life with you. **R**

We bring to mind those persons among us in need of healing. Hear our prayers offered in faith that you already know the names of all who seek your touch:_____. **R**

Though we remember we are dust and to dust we shall return, we remember that we are your precious dust. **Amen.**

Texts: Genesis 12:1-4a   Psalm 121   Romans 4:1-5, 13-17   John 3:1-17 or Matthew 17:1-9

3rd Sunday in Lent

Responsive Sentence for the Sundays in Lent:
    The day of the Lord is coming: **He abounds in steadfast love.**

Heavenly Father, you know how we, like all generations before us, doubt your nearness. We would test you like the Israelites at Meribah. Because we cannot see you any more than the air we need to breathe, you sent your Son and Holy Spirit, because we need you, even more than air, for a real life. **R**

O Rock of our Salvation, help us make a joyful noise with songs of praise and thanksgiving, for you are the LORD, and a great King above all gods. In your hands are the depths of the earth, the sea and the mountain top. You are our God and we are the sheep of your pasture. **R**

Lord Jesus Christ, you are the nearness of God in our lives. You know our plight in the flesh. You died for us, the ungodly, while we were yet sinners. We boast of your love for us, because you turn our sufferings into endurance and character and hope. **R**

Lord Jesus, your food for life was to do your Father's will. You give living water to all who thirst to know God as the Father unlike any earthly father, for He sent you to us with living water in hand. Quench our thirst for the only God who is God. **R**

We bring before you those who suffer among us with illnesses of all sorts. Until we all receive our new lives in the kingdom yet to come, bring relief to those among us who are in pain or distress of any kind: _____. **R**

Though we remember we are dust and to dust we shall return, we remember that we are your precious dust. **Amen.**

Texts: Exodus 17:1-7   Psalm 95   Romans 5:1-11   John 4:5-42

4th Sunday in Lent

Responsive Sentence for the Sundays in Lent:
    The day of the Lord is coming: **He abounds in steadfast love.**

Lord God, you sent Samuel to anoint David in front of his brothers, and your Spirit came mightily upon him all the days of his life. Anoint us with your Holy Spirit, that we may serve you all the days of our lives. **R**

Lord Jesus Christ, you are our Good Shepherd. Even as the Psalmist talked *about* you in his Psalm, until he started talking *with* you, so train us to learn from his example. Become for us not only the subject of our holy conversation, but also our dearest confidant and companion. **R**

Holy Spirit, help us understand what is pleasing to the Lord so that we may be children of the light. Wake up our sleeping spirits so that the light of Christ may shine on us and through us. **R**

Lord Jesus Christ, you are the Light of the World. Even as you opened the eyes of the blind, open our eyes to see your presence everywhere, and give us the courage to confess our faith boldly, like one who knows whom to thank. **R**

Great Physician, the infirmities of all people are subject to you and your word. If it be your will, heal those with special needs whom we name silently or aloud before you: _____ . **R**

Though we remember we are dust and to dust we shall return, we remember that we are your precious dust. **Amen.**

Texts: 1 Samuel 16:1-13   Psalm 23   Ephesians 5:8-14   John 9:1-41

5th Sunday in Lent

Responsive Sentence for the Sundays in Lent:
    The day of the Lord is coming: **He abounds in steadfast love.**

Heavenly Father, sometimes we sense that our lives are very dry, like the dry bones in Ezekiel's vision. We need your Holy breath, your Holy Spirit, so that all of our other senses may be keen to your presence, your work, your love among us. **R**

Lord Jesus Christ, hear us when we cry to you. Lord Jesus Christ, may we hear you when you speak to us. **R**

Holy Spirit, live in us with Jesus Christ, so that He who raised Jesus from the dead will live in us and be our God. **R**

Jesus, you have seen the sadness of all of us who mourn in Mary's weeping over Lazarus. We hold to your promise that all of us will rise again, as we hear you call our names. **R**

We rejoice over all the glories of this day, and thank you for your goodness to us all. Help us see the needs of others, help us hear their cries, and help us be your helping hands. **R**

Those among us who are ill know that they are named before you out of love and compassion. Hear us as we name them now: _____ . **R**

Though we remember we are dust and to dust we shall return, we remember that we are your precious dust. **Amen.**

Texts: Ezekiel 37:1-14   Psalm 130   Romans 8:6-11   John 11:1-45

6th Sunday in Lent
Sunday of the Passion, Palm Sunday

Responsive Sentence for the Sunday of the Passion:
   We trust in you O LORD: **You are our God.**

Lord God, our Heavenly Father and Helper, open our ears that we may hear you as clearly as Isaiah did. Teach us to listen more intently to your Word than we do to the sounds of the world. When we hear, may we obey and rejoice with those who sang you into Jerusalem. **R**

Lord Jesus Christ, you emptied yourself for us. You set aside the glories of heaven and came to earth as the only Son of God. You were obedient unto death, even death on a cross. We confess that you are our Lord, the glory of God the Father. **R**

Holy Spirit, even as you were with Christ at His trial, be with us in our trials that we may not fear the forces of this world that can only inflict death. You remembered whose you were. You are the resurrection and the life. **R**

Lord Jesus Christ when we cry out in joy, hear our song as a song of thanksgiving. When we cry out in despair, remind us to commit our cause and our spirit into your hands. **R**

On this Sunday of the Passion, remember the suffering of those among us who need to know your love for them surpasses all human understanding: _____. **R**

Though we remember we are dust and to dust we shall return, we remember that we are your precious dust. **Amen.**

Texts for the Liturgy of the Palms: Matthew 21:1-11   Psalm 118:1-2, 19-29

Texts for the Liturgy of the Passion: Isaiah 50:4-9a   Psalm 31:9-16   Philippians 2:5-11   Matthew 26:14—27:66 or Matthew 27:11-54

YEAR A

Maundy Thursday

Responsive Sentence for Maundy Thursday:
   Let us love one another: **As Christ has loved us.**

Lord Jesus Christ, we often see Peter's reluctance to have you wash his feet as our hesitation in all things spiritual, for you end up touching the physical. You end up touching us. Give us the courage to let you touch us, head to toe. **R**

Lord Jesus Christ, you command us to wash each other's feet. The indignity never ends! Yet we know what to ask. Give us the courage to touch one another, for the sake of healing, head to toe. **R**

Holy Spirit, courage-giver, teach us how to bend our knees, fold our hands, and lift up our eyes to the loving Father, who cared so much that He sent us His Son to die for us. We cannot match the humiliation of Jesus, but we give thanks for His holy work on our behalf. **R**

Heavenly Father, you single us out for love of such depth and beauty that we can scarcely stand it, or understand it. For the love of us, you gave your only Son! **R**

Your new commandment, Lord Jesus, is to love one another as you have loved us. When you kneel before us, towel in hand, we know we are not worthy. Wash us anyway. Make us humble. Help us be each other's keeper. **R**

Though we remember we are dust and to dust we shall return, we remember that we are your precious dust. **Amen.**

Texts: Exodus 12:1-4 [5-10] 11-14   Psalm 116:1-2, 12-19   1 Corinthians 11:23-26   John 13:1-17, 31b-35

Good Friday

Responsive Sentence for Good Friday:
   God of the ages: **You love us.**

Heavenly Father, the pain of Good Friday is rebellion against you. You sent a Son, your one and only, and they crucified Him because all generations want a God unlike the God who is you. It is our sin to want you to be bold and brave, strong and militant, rather than a God filled with so much mercy and love. **R**

Holy Spirit, you were there in power, giving Jesus the will to die for the likes of us. We do not know what you whispered in His heart, or what you reminded Him of in His memory. We only know He did not stop the awful crucifixion, which was His alone to cancel. **R**

Lord Jesus Christ, we see ourselves in Pontius Pilate, your judge. He was trapped, like we are, dealing with you on this earth where justice so often means punishment. He did not know how to say "no" to death. **R**

Forgive us, Father, Son and Holy Spirit. We do not know all that we have done. It is not our ignorance which emboldens us to ask for forgiveness. It is your death, your love, your power and your mercy. And more than all of this, it is our desire to be with you forever. **R**

Into your hands we commend all who do not know you, but need you. Help us ache for their discovery of a God so good that He loves even those of us who walk away. **R**

Though we remember we are dust and to dust we shall return, we remember that we are your precious dust. **Amen.**

Texts: Isaiah 52:13—53:12   Psalm 22   Hebrews 10:16-25 or Hebrews 4:14-16; 5:7-9   John 18:1—19:42

YEAR A

Easter Day
Resurrection of Our Lord

Responsive Sentence for the Sundays of Easter:
   Set our minds on heavenly things: **Fill us with your joy.**

Lord Jesus Christ, ordained by God as Judge of the living and the dead, you are Lord of all. Resurrected Lord, fill us with your grace for we are your people. **R**

We give thanks to you, Lord God, for you are good, and your mercy endures forever. **R**

Lord Jesus Christ, preacher, healer, first person raised from death forever, you are ordained by God, and from you we receive the forgiveness of sins. **R**

Lord Jesus Christ, visit our tombs, remove our headstones that oppress us even now, and become our chief cornerstone, that we may proclaim by deed and voice with Mary Magdalene: "I have seen the Lord!" **R**

All worlds know of your power, Lord God, and sing your praises, for you alone are the Holy One. Hear us, even now, as we join your heavenly chorus. **R**

Resurrected Lord and Great Physician, we boldly bring before you those in need of your loving power: _____. **R**

Help us listen closely to your Word, even as you listen to our prayers. **Amen.**

Texts: Acts 10:34-43 or Jeremiah 31:1-6   Psalm 118:1-2, 14-24   Colossians 3:1-4 or Acts 10:34-43   John 20:1-18 or Matthew 28:1-10

2nd Sunday of Easter

Responsive Sentence for the Sundays of Easter:
    Set our minds on heavenly things: **Fill us with your joy.**

Heavenly Father, even as you promised King David that the Messiah would be his descendant, King David prophesied that you would raise the Messiah from the dead. We thank you for keeping your promise and fulfilling your prophet's word. **R**

Heavenly Father, protect us from the pit of death with your strong right arm and raise us up like Jesus. Be our path of life, our joy, our confidence for an everlasting future with you. **R**

By your great mercy, Heavenly Father, you give us a new birth of expectation through Jesus Christ, the very salvation of our souls. Though tested with trials, may our faith always honor and praise you. **R**

We yearn, Lord Jesus Christ, to hear you say, "Peace be with you." With nail-pierced hands extended, give us the ear of faith to hear you say that we are also your beloved disciples. **R**

Holy Spirit, very God at work in our hearts, minds and souls, fill us with trust in the Word, love for one another, and the very presence of Christ in our lives. **R**

Our world suffers, Lord God, from disbelief in your presence and your promises. Give us a voice to speak clearly, live rightly and care for this precious earth from which we were born, to which we return and from which you will raise us up. **R**

Lord Jesus, you know all among us who suffer from loneliness, disease, wavering faith and losses of all kinds. Hear us as we name our kindred, friends and even our enemies who need your touch: _____. **R**

Help us listen closely to your Word, even as you listen to our prayers. **Amen.**

Texts: Acts 2:14a, 22-32   Psalm 16   1 Peter 1:3-9   John 20:19-31

YEAR A

3rd Sunday of Easter

Responsive Sentence for the Sundays of Easter:
    Set our minds on heavenly things: **Fill us with your joy.**

Lord and Messiah, Jesus Christ, we rejoice in our baptisms in your name. With our sins forgiven may the gift of the Holy Spirit keep us faithful all the days of our lives. **R**

Heavenly Father, we know we are not able to repay you for all your goodness to us. We are your unworthy but happy servants. Hear our songs of thanksgiving in the presence of all your people. **R**

Heavenly Father, we revere your name for we have been died for by your Son. You sent Him to earth for us, and you raised Him from the dead. Our faith and expectation for eternal life are gifts of love from you. **R**

Lord Jesus Christ, our hearts burn within us when we celebrate a Holy Communion with you. May the Holy Spirit continue to make Christ known to us in the breaking of the bread. **R**

Though we study the Word for a lifetime, Lord Jesus, we still need the Holy Spirit to prod us, tickle us, and sometimes scold us to make that leap of faith into the loving arms of the Heavenly Father. **R**

Before you all the complaints, worries, illnesses and problems of the world melt like wax from your holy light. Give us courage to believe that you lovingly care for all whom we name aloud or in our hearts who have special needs: _____. **R**

Help us listen closely to your Word, even as you listen to our prayers. **Amen.**

Texts: Acts 2:14a, 36-41   Psalm 116:1-4, 12-19   1 Peter 1:17-23   Luke 24:13-35

4th Sunday of Easter

Responsive Sentence for the Sundays of Easter:
    Set our minds on heavenly things: **Fill us with your joy.**

Lord Jesus Christ, as we break bread and pray the prayer you've taught us to pray, fill us with glad and generous hearts that our family of faith may grow, the needs of others may be served, and a sense of awe may come upon us through your love. **R**

Heavenly Father, when rivers flood, tsunamis kill, hurricanes rage and the earth quakes, remind us of your green pastures, your still waters, your comforting shepherd's rod, your presence in our darkest valley, your table prepared, your cup poured full, and your eternal dwelling place opened for us so that our souls may be quieted and restored. **R**

Holy Spirit of Almighty God, when our hearts are troubled and we feel wrongly accused or punished, remind us of the healing wounds of Christ, the shepherd and guardian of our souls. **R**

Lord Jesus, our Good Shepherd, give us an ear to hear our names being called to come home to your fold, that we may live lives of abundant courage and faith. **R**

Lord Jesus, gate keeper, open up all that we've locked out from you out of fear, selfishness or shame. Come into our hearts as we come into your fold, for your sake, for our sake, and for the sake of one another. **R**

We bring before you the needs of the nations, the earth, the communities and neighborhoods of all your people. Help us see and respond in love as you would have us do. **R**

Among us both near and far away are persons who suffer terrible disease, misfortune, and injustice. As we name these concerns and people, increase our caring love: _____. **R**

Help us listen closely to your Word, even as you listen to our prayers. **Amen.**

Texts: Acts 2:42-47   Psalm 23   1 Peter 2:19-25   John 10:1-10

YEAR A

5th Sunday of Easter

Responsive Sentence for the Sundays of Easter:
   Set our minds on heavenly things: **Fill us with your joy.**

Heavenly Father, even as Stephen could see the Lord Jesus Christ seated at your right hand, fill us with courage to look heavenward when all the world rejects our witness. **R**

Heavenly Father, you are our rock of refuge. Our times are in your hands. Guide us with your steadfast love even as you listen to our prayers. **R**

Living Stone, Lord Jesus Christ, be our cornerstone. You have chosen us to be your people, and we have tasted your goodness and have received your mercy. **R**

Lord Jesus, Son of the Father, you speak of the Father's house as your home and our home. Be the Way, the Truth and the Life for each of us. **R**

Holy Spirit, help us understand Jesus' good news that He is in the Father and the Father is in Him. May we rejoice to know that Jesus was always about the Father's business. **R**

All the world seems to be at odds, Lord Jesus Christ, unable to accept your deep involvement in our daily lives. Do not let us sink into the abyss of disbelief. **R**

Heavenly One, Father, Son and Holy Spirit, care for those among us with special needs. Be father and mother, sister and brother, friend and healer to all whom we now name before you: _____. **R**

Help us listen closely to your Word, even as you listen to our prayers. **Amen.**

Texts: Acts 7:55-60   Psalm 31:1-5, 15-16   1 Peter 2:2-10   John 14:1-14

6th Sunday of Easter

Responsive Sentence for the Sundays of Easter:
    Set our minds on heavenly things: **Fill us with your joy.**

Heavenly Father, giver of our life and breath, you need nothing from any of us for all belongs to you. Yet we are your offspring, your beloved ones, and you yearn for us to turn toward you with faith and devotion. **R**

We bless you, O Lord Our Father, with our very God-given souls, for they come from you, and you cherish everyone of us as your child. You raised Jesus from the dead, and will have Him be our loving judge at the end of time. **R**

How great thou art, Lord God, to hear the petitions of all your people as though each of us is in a private audience with you. **R**

We appeal to you, Heavenly Father, through Jesus Christ, who desires to bring us all to you. He suffered for all of us, for the righteous and the unrighteous, out of great love for you, and out of great love for us. Your loving Son gives us our worthiness and makes us your children. **R**

Lord Jesus Christ, we rejoice in your promise that all who love you will also be loved by the Father. **R**

Loving God and Father of us all, we bring before you our brothers and sisters with needs beyond our capacity to help. Be their healer, mentor, friend and holy God, even as we name them aloud and commit them into your care: _____. **R**

Help us listen closely to your Word, even as you listen to our prayers. **Amen.**

Texts: Acts 17:22-31   Psalm 66:8-20   1 Peter 3:13-22   John 14:15-21

YEAR A

7th Sunday of Easter

Responsive Sentence for the Sundays of Easter:
    Set our minds on heavenly things: **Fill us with your joy.**

Heavenly Father, you, alone, know the day and the hour of all creation. Set our minds and hearts on being your faithful laborers. Help us work your heavenly will all the days of our lives. **R**

Lord God, as the Psalmist sees you ride upon the cloud with no need of wing nor motor, so our Lord Jesus Christ rose and disappeared causing the disciples to gaze upward. Help us to lower our eyes to the tasks at hand, until the Lord returns. **R**

Father of orphans and protector of widows, you care for all of us in need. You invite us to sing praises to you, for your sanctuary is awesome and you give power and strength to your people. **R**

Lord God, you test us and invite us to rejoice in our sufferings with Christ among us. Help us cast all our cares upon you, for you carry them away when we let them go. **R**

Our adversary, the devil, prowls around like a roaring lion seeking to devour us. Help us to resist him, for he is our enemy. **R**

Lord Jesus Christ, you have been given the keys to the kingdom of heaven, eternal life. To know the Father, the one true God, is eternal life, and toward that goal we yearn to be your disciples and friends. **R**

Lord Jesus Christ, when we hear you in prayer to the Heavenly Father on our behalf, we pause with the greatest pause possible, marveling over your deep love for each of us. **R**

Before you we bring the names of persons precious to us, but even more precious to you, no matter how deep our love may be. Care for them as only you can do: _____. **R**

Help us listen closely to your Word, even as you listen to our prayers. **Amen.**

Texts: Acts 1:6-14   Psalm 68:1-10, 32-35   1 Peter 4:12-14; 5:6-11   John 17:1-11

The Day of Pentecost

Responsive Sentence for the Day of Pentecost:
    We pray in the Spirit: **Jesus is Lord.**

Holy Spirit, God Almighty, pour yourself out and into our souls, that we may see the presence of Christ among us, the care of the Holy Father for us, and the faith of our children, and our children's children, alive, growing, and well. **R**

Almighty God, you give us the skill and the will to work your miracles for one another. Whether we say the kind word, the healing word, or the prophetic word, you let us touch each other's souls and bodies with your Holy Spirit. **R**

As long as we live we sing to you, Lord God, for you have filled the world with marvels, beauty, and the wisdom of seasons. At all times and in all the seasons of our lives, be present, Holy Spirit, be present. **R**

When we see your hands, nail-pierced for us, and hear you say "Peace be with you," we know you have forgiven us our sins, breathed your Holy Spirit upon us, and have invited us to forgive one another. **R**

Help us see and hear and sense all who worship with us at this holy hour in this holy place. Angels, archangels, all the company of heaven, the church which gathered on the first Day of Pentecost, and the church triumphant fill every space in every pew, to cheer us on as your latest and current church militant. **R**

We remember the needs of the living who seek your healing, that our brief season on the earth may be extended and made whole. We also remember the saints who have lived among us in our time and place. We name all aloud, some for healing, some with thanksgiving, all witnesses to your love: _____. **R**

Father, Son and Holy Spirit, one God, continue to use us as your living saints.
Amen.

Texts: Acts 2:1-21 or Numbers 11:24-30   Psalm 104:24-34, 35b   1 Corinthians 12:3b-13 or Acts 2:1-21 John 20:19-23 or John 7:37-39

YEAR A

The Holy Trinity
First Sunday after Pentecost

Responsive Sentence for the Holy Trinity:
>   You are always with us: **To the end of time.**

Creator God, when you speak worlds happen, light blinks darkness away, life is born and nothingness is all gone. Speak to the void in each of us that we may be formed in your image, according to your likeness, for your holy purposes. **R**

God of love and peace, fill us with the grace of Christ that the communion of the Holy Spirit may always be shared among us. **R**

Heavenly Father, our own Creator, with the Psalmist we wonder why you are so mindful of us, so in love with us, and have given us so much. Keep us from making you a very small God by doubting that you care about every detail of our lives. **R**

Lord Jesus Christ, cure our doubting hearts and use us as your disciples. **R**

Jesus, all authority from heaven and earth has been given to you. You command us to make disciples, baptize, teach and obey. Give us the will to let your will be done. **R**

Father, Son and Holy Spirit, God in three persons, blessed Trinity, you make us, redeem us and love us. We can not ask for anything more. **R**

We recognize our physical needs as well as our spiritual lethargy. Be for us the Great Physician as we name those among us in need of healing and hope:_____. **R**

Father, Son, and Holy Spirit, one God, continue to use us as your living saints. **Amen.**

Texts: Genesis 1:1—2:4a   Psalm 8   2 Corinthians 13:11-13   Matthew 28:16-20

Time after Pentecost, Lectionary 8A

Responsive Sentence for the Sundays after Pentecost:
    Prince of Peace: **Come, Lord Jesus, come.**

Heavenly Father, you have promised us: "I will not forget you." In the day of suffering remind us that you have inscribed our names on the palms of your hands, and you can no more forget us than a mother forgets she nursed her child. **R**

Holy Spirit, quiet our souls when our misplaced hope has been dashed, and bring us back to trust and hope only in you. **R**

Lord Jesus, as your servants, we have been entrusted to be stewards of the mysteries of God. Help us look forward to the day when you return to lighten things now hidden in the darkness, and to disclose the purposes of the heart. **R**

Remove worry from our hearts, Holy Spirit, that we may make more room for you. **R**

Lord of the lilies of the field and the birds of the air, give us nerve to strive first for the kingdom of God, so that worry itself, becomes unworthy of our time. **R**

We bring before you the names of friends and family, foes and strangers, that you, in your mercy, may make us all whole: _____. **R**

Your steadfast love is your daily gift for our daily need. Thank you, loving Lord. **Amen.**

Texts: Isaiah 49:8-16a   Psalm 131   1 Corinthians 4:1-5   Matthew 6:24-34

Dates: May 24 – May 28

YEAR A

Time after Pentecost, Lectionary 9A

Responsive Sentence for the Sundays after Pentecost:
   Prince of Peace: **Come, Lord Jesus, come.**

Heavenly Father, forever using your Word as the touchstone of your heart, help us hear what you are saying to us out of love, so that we may give thanks for our every blessing. **R**

Holy Spirit, we commit our very spirit to your greatness, knowing that you are able to hold us safe from human plots, malicious gossip, and evil intent from all the forces of the evil one. **R**

Lord Jesus Christ, grace bearer, giver of every good and gracious gift, help us rely on your mercy, for our deeds fail us everyday. **R**

Heavenly Father, who art in heaven, your will is for us to love your Son and to love one another, as companions on a pilgrimage to your kingdom beyond this earth. **R**

When the floods come, and the fires destroy, and war is rampant, and all that is physical is shown to be a fragile illusion, remind us, Holy Spirit, that you are indestructible, and beyond death. **R**

Lord God, our rock and fortress, your goodness is abundant, as you hear every supplication of our hearts. Hear us, now, as we pray for those in need: _____. **R**

Your steadfast love is your daily gift for our daily need. Thank you, loving Lord. **Amen.**

Texts: Deuteronomy 11:18-21, 26-28 or Genesis 6:9-22; 7:24; 8:14-19   Psalm 31:1-5, 19-24 or Psalm 46 Romans 1:16-17; 3:22b-28 [29-31]   Matthew 7:21-29

Dates: May 29 – June 4

Time after Pentecost, Lectionary 10A

Responsive Sentence for the Sundays after Pentecost:
　　Prince of Peace:　　　　　　　　**Come, Lord Jesus, come.**

Heavenly Father, you desire the personal gift of love over the perpetual offering plate, because true love is far more costly than money. Enable us to give heart to the brokenhearted, hope to the those in despair, love to one wounded by hate, and joy to the one who has forgotten how to sing. **R**

Holy Spirit, as we learn to say "Thank you, Lord" you have taught us to understand that we are in deep debt to you, yet all you've ever wanted from us is Love. **R**

Lord God Almighty, able to do what you have promised, give us ears to hear you calling us to be careful caretakers of this earth, and all granted breath upon it. **R**

Your strong word, Jesus Christ, to the desperate, is always: "Take heart." Keep us from the sin of despair. **R**

If in this life only we have hope, we are most to be pitied. Nevertheless, we presume upon your love and power to heal and help those whom we name before you: _____. **R**

Your steadfast love is your daily gift for our daily need. Thank you, loving Lord. **Amen.**

Texts:　Hosea 5:15—6:6 or Genesis 12:1-9　Psalm 50:7-15 or Psalm 33:1-12　Romans 4:13-25　Matthew 9:9-13, 18-26

Dates:　June 5 – June 11

YEAR A

Time after Pentecost, Lectionary 11A

Responsive Sentence for the Sundays after Pentecost:
　　Prince of Peace:　　　　　　　　　**Come, Lord Jesus, come.**

Heavenly Father, even as you called the Israelites to a Passover Feast that would begin their journey into the wilderness for freedom's sake, so you have called us to dine with you in a Holy Communion, the foretaste of the feast to come. **R**

Holy Spirit, inspire us to sing old and new songs of praise, remembering our great traditions and rejoicing anew with hearts and voices filled with mirth. **R**

Lord Jesus Christ, Paul instructs us to boast in our sufferings, for they are an indication that we will share in the glory of God. **R**

Our Father, you let your Son die for us while we were still sinners, knowing that His death would become the one thing necessary for our redemption. **R**

Jesus, Good Shepherd, as you shepherd us to hear the good news regarding the nearness of your kingdom, help us care about the harvest of love-starved souls surrounding us everyday. **R**

We bring before you those in need of the special attention of the Good Shepherd: _____. **R**

Your steadfast love is your daily gift for our daily need. Thank you, loving Lord. **Amen.**

Texts:　Exodus 19:2-8a or Genesis 18:1-15 [21:1-7]　Psalm 100 or Psalm 116:1-2, 12-19　Romans 5:1-8　Matthew 9:35—10:8 [9-23]

Dates:　June 12 – June 18

Time after Pentecost, Lectionary 12A

Responsive Sentence for the Sundays after Pentecost:
   Prince of Peace: **Come, Lord Jesus, come.**

Lord God Almighty, even as you enticed and overpowered Jeremiah, because you test the righteous, so help us commit ourselves to trust your holy will over our own lives. **R**

Fill us with zeal, Holy Spirit, and fill us with love for your church, that we may share in your steadfast love for this world. **R**

Lord Jesus Christ, we have been baptized into your death, that we might be raised from the dead to walk in newness of life. Free us from our bondage to sin, that we may be united with you on the day of resurrection. **R**

Make us your trustworthy servants, Lord, and acknowledge us before our Father in heaven as your loving children. **R**

As we learn to bear the cross of Christ, following the way of Jesus, comfort us with your many promises of eternal joy in your presence. **R**

We remember those among us who are bearing problems and illnesses that need the attention of Our Lord Jesus Christ. Be the guardian and healer of those whom we name before you: _____. **R**

Your steadfast love is your daily gift for our daily need. Thank you loving Lord. **Amen.**

Texts: Jeremiah 20:7-13 or Genesis 21:8-21   Psalm 69:7-10 [11-15] 16-18 or Psalm 86:1-10, 16-17
Romans 6:1b-11   Matthew 10:24-39

Dates: June 19 – June 25

Time after Pentecost, Lectionary 13A

Responsive Sentence for the Sundays after Pentecost:
   Prince of Peace: **Come, Lord Jesus, come.**

Heavenly Father, you have used prophets, priests and kings to enter human history. Give us the wisdom to hear your voice in their proclamations, to obey your will, and to give thanks for your daily intervention against all that is evil. **R**

Your steadfast love, Lord God, never gives up. You keep your promises forever. Your faithfulness is our hope and certainty that you are involved in every generation, in every family, in every living soul. **R**

Holy Spirit, increase our desire to grow in the faith as children of the Heavenly Father, for we know that such sanctification leads to eternal life in Christ Jesus our Lord. **R**

Lord Jesus Christ, you tell us to welcome you and the Heavenly Father by welcoming those who speak your Word in truth. Open our ears to your Word, our hearts to your messenger, our wills to your superior will and our futures to your care. **R**

Holy Spirit, the world's problems are overwhelming, and we are not able to list every malady, need or injustice. Be our counselor, and when opportunity to help is evident, give us courage to act. **R**

Lord, you know all who stand before you in faith and in need. You, alone, see the saints alive in both the church triumphant and the church militant. We remember with joy those who have preceded us in the faith, and as we name them in our hearts, we also name aloud all those whom we know with special needs: _____. **R**

Your steadfast love is your daily gift for our daily need. Thank you, loving Lord. **Amen.**

Texts: Jeremiah 28:5-9 or Genesis 22:1-14   Psalm 89:1-4, 15-18 or Psalm 13   Romans 6:12-23   Matthew 10:40-42

Dates: June 26 – July 2

Time after Pentecost, Lectionary 14A

Responsive Sentence for the Sundays after Pentecost:
　　Prince of Peace:　　　　　　　　**Come, Lord Jesus, come.**

Heavenly Father, you sent our king, Jesus, into Jerusalem on a donkey, for he came in boundless peace. Help us us understand the limits of a war horse, however it is built, for you command peace to the nations, from sea to sea, from rivers' ends to the ends of the earth. **R**

Gracious Lord, slow to anger, lover of each of us, we bless you for all your holy works. Your glory, splendor, and power endure forever, for you are faithful in all your deeds and words. **R**

Holy Spirit, Comforter, we do not understand our own actions. So often we cannot do the good we want to do, for sin lives within each of us. Rescue us from this body of death through the living presence of the greater life in us, even Jesus Christ, Our Lord. **R**

Jesus, you invite us to come to you with the heaviest of our burdens. Your yoke is built for two, and you always pull the greater weight. Help us let you do what you want to do for us. **R**

We remember the departed saints of our own time, who seemed to be stronger in the faith than we are. We remember the departed sinners of our own time, who still make our lives very difficult. We name them, silently, in our hearts, and commit them into your care. **R**

These bodies of ours are a constant consternation, yet we know this life on earth is a gracious gift from you, and we wish for you to prolong it as long as you think best. Hear our prayers for those in need of healing: _____. **R**

Your steadfast love is your daily gift for our daily need. Thank you, loving Lord. **Amen.**

Texts:　Zechariah 9:9-12 or Genesis 24:34-38, 42-49, 58-67　Psalm 145:8-14 or Psalm 45:10-17 or Song of Solomon 2:8-13　Romans 7:15-25a　Matthew 11:16-19, 25-30

Dates:　July 3 – July 9

YEAR A

Time after Pentecost, Lectionary 15A

Responsive Sentence for the Sundays after Pentecost:
  Prince of Peace: **Come, Lord Jesus, come.**

Heavenly Father, your mighty Word—spoken, written or meditated upon, is dynamite power. Your Word does not return to you empty, but accomplishes your work. Speak to us and work on us until your Word takes root, feeds us full and brings peace for all of us. **R**

Holy Spirit, you gave the Psalmists words of praise and love of your law. Make your Word a lamp to our feet and light for our path. **R**

Lord Jesus Christ, life in you sets us free from the law of sin and the law of death, and enables us to walk according to the Spirit. Help us set our minds on the things of the Spirit, from whom comes life and peace. **R**

Lord Jesus, cultivate our hearts like a gardener cultivates the soil, that we may be receptive to your Word, and bear fruit for your kingdom. **R**

We know that reaching out to others regarding your work and love among us is daunting to the poor in Spirit. Give us the will and skill to be your persistent evangelists. **R**

We bring before you the needs of countries, kingdoms, states, counties, towns and neighborhoods, wherever there is conflict or disaster. Known to us are family and friends who also need your healing touch. Hear us as we name them in our hearts or aloud before your gathered congregation: _____. **R**

Your steadfast love is your daily gift for our daily need. Thank you, loving Lord. **Amen.**

Texts: Isaiah 55:10-13 or Genesis 25:19-34   Psalm 65:[1-8] 9-13 or Psalm 119:105-112   Romans 8:1-11   Matthew 13:1-9, 18-23

Dates: July 10 – July 16

Time after Pentecost, Lectionary 16A

Responsive Sentence for the Sundays after Pentecost:
    Prince of Peace: **Come, Lord Jesus, come.**

Lord God, only God, there are no other gods. Rock of ages, Redeemer, Sanctifier, make us your glad witnesses. **R**

Gracious and merciful God, teach us your way that we may walk in your truth with an undivided heart. We revere your steadfast love and holy name. **R**

Holy Spirit, teach us to be your children. As beloved children of God, give us the voice to joyfully call out "Abba! Father!", for you have made us your heirs and joint heirs with Christ. **R**

Lord Jesus Christ, you have sown the seeds of faith in our hearts, yet we know that weeds from the evil one remain in our lives. Forgive us our sin, and protect us from the enemy. **R**

The needy among us, O Lord, includes all of us, for we are not able to come to you by our own strength. But we hear your call, we feel your pull and we ask for your help to obey your command to speak with you honestly about all of our needs. Hear us as pray for one another: _____. **R**

Your steadfast love is your daily gift for our daily need. Thank you, loving Lord. **Amen.**

Texts: Isaiah 44:6-8 or Wisdom of Solomon 12:13, 16-19 or Genesis 28:10-19a   Psalm 86:11-17 or Psalm 139:1-12, 23-24   Romans 8:12-25   Matthew 13:24-30, 36-43

Dates: July 17 – July 23

Time after Pentecost, Lectionary 17A

Responsive Sentence for the Sundays after Pentecost:
    Prince of Peace: **Come, Lord Jesus, come.**

Heavenly Father, help us to pray the prayer of Solomon, that we might have an understanding mind, able to discern between good and evil. **R**

With the Psalmist we know that your decrees are good for us, and your commandments are a gift. Make your face shine on us, and help us keep your statutes. **R**

Holy Spirit, when we do not know how to pray rightly, intercede for us with sighs too deep for words, for our pain is often too deep to utter, and our understanding is so humanly limited. **R**

Lord Jesus Christ, you speak of the kingdom of God as a seed, like yeast, like a treasure in a field, a pearl of great price, a net filled with fish of every kind. Help us sense how valuable your kingdom is for our everyday lives. **R**

Lord of the resurrection, you have already harvested saints from the past, who loved you as best they could. Help us remember that all who have died in the faith are alive in you. **R**

Hear our prayers for the concerns of the world, our country, our community and our congregation. We know that all of us have special needs, yet we name aloud a few among us who have more urgent needs: _____. **R**

Your steadfast love is your daily gift for our daily need. Thank you, loving Lord. **Amen.**

Texts: 1 Kings 3:5-12 or Genesis 29:15-28   Psalm 119:129-136 or Psalm 105:1-11, 45b or Psalm 128   Romans 8:26-39   Matthew 13:31-33, 44-52

Dates: July 24 – July 30

Time after Pentecost, Lectionary 18A

Responsive Sentence for the Sundays after Pentecost:
    Prince of Peace: **Come, Lord Jesus, come.**

Heavenly Father, your everlasting covenant with us is your steadfast love. You will not stop loving us. You will be present with us regardless of our weakness, in spite of our sinfulness, despite our faithlessness. You do not abandon any of us. **R**

Lord God, slow to anger and abounding in steadfast love, as you have compassion on all that you have made, give us the wisdom to look for you, speak with you, and call upon your name. **R**

Lord Jesus Christ, even as Paul is in anguish over his fellow Jews, help us care for every person, regardless of faith, or lack of faith. We remember that you work through history, especially the history of the Israelites, for whom we give our thanks. **R**

Lord Jesus Christ, in the feeding of the multitude, help us remember that you feed us also with your word, with your gifts, with your very life and Holy Spirit. As you fill us with your abundance, remind us of all those who need a kind word or deed from us. **R**

Hear us pray for those in need, and give us the strength to act upon the very help we ask from you, that we may generously reach out to those we now name before you: _____. **R**

Your steadfast love is your daily gift for our daily need. Thank you, loving Lord. **Amen.**

Texts: Isaiah 55:1-5 or Genesis 32:22-31   Psalm 145:8-9, 14-21 or Psalm 17:1-7, 15   Romans 9:1-5
Matthew 14:13-21

Dates: July 31 – August 6

YEAR A

Time after Pentecost, Lectionary 19A

Responsive Sentence for the Sundays after Pentecost:
    Prince of Peace: **Come, Lord Jesus, come.**

Heavenly Father, give us the ability of Elijah to listen to your direct questions to each of us, and give us courage to hear your commands to be of service to you. **R**

Your steadfast love, Lord God, is matched by your faithfulness. May peace and righteousness result in our lives because of your presence among us. **R**

Jesus, first to be resurrected from the dead by God, never to die again, we confess that you are our Lord. Make beautiful our feet as we seek to spread the good news of your salvation. **R**

Holy Spirit, thank you for reminding us not to be afraid when Jesus appears to us with grace, love, compassion, or rescue. **R**

We remember that we are to be caretakers of this earth, out of which we were born, and to which we return. Make us your good stewards of the earth, the sky, all waters and every living thing, both honoring and preserving your creation. **R**

The fragile lives of all of us need your constant attention, your Holy Spirit, and your healing, over and over again. Hear us as we name those with special needs: _____. **R**

Your steadfast love is your daily gift for our daily need. Thank you, loving Lord. **Amen.**

Texts: 1 Kings 19:9-18 or Genesis 37:1-4, 12-28   Psalm 85:8-13 or Psalm 105:1-6, 16-22, 45b   Romans 10:5-15   Matthew 14:22-33

Dates: August 7 – August 13

Time after Pentecost, Lectionary 20A

Responsive Sentence for the Sundays after Pentecost:
    Prince of Peace: **Come, Lord Jesus, come.**

Heavenly God and Father of us all, we are grateful that you call us to work for justice, to gather weekly in your house of prayer, and to expect new people to join with us in joyful worship. **R**

Gracious God, your face shines upon us, and we are known as your saving help among all nations. Even as you have blessed us, may all the people of the earth praise you. **R**

Lord God, you call each of us your own. You, alone, give human beings the desire to give mercy and gifts of love to one another. **R**

Holy Spirit, purify our hearts that we may be kept from wrongdoing. Put a seal upon our lips when we are tempted to speak unkindly, to lie, deceive or deny your constant presence. **R**

The saints who have preceded us in the faith still inspire us to hold fast to your Word, to trust your Holy Spirit, and to expect a great reunion in the life to come. Hear us as we name those special ones who have joined your church triumphant: _____. **R**

The needs of all the earth, the victims of every land, and the illnesses of everyone are all known to you. Yet we are bold to name the ones we know most personally, and ask for your help and healing: _____. **R**

Your steadfast love is your daily gift for our daily need. Thank you, loving Lord. **Amen.**

Texts: Isaiah 56:1, 6-8 or Genesis 45:1-15   Psalm 67 or Psalm 133   Romans 11:1-2a, 29-32   Matthew 15:[10-20] 21-28

Dates: August 14 – August 20

YEAR A

Time after Pentecost, Lectionary 21A

Responsive Sentence for the Sundays after Pentecost:
   Prince of Peace: **Come, Lord Jesus, come.**

Heavenly Father, your prophet, Isaiah, reminds us of your mighty deeds, your promises of light for today's work, and everlasting deliverance when the earth wears out like a garment. **R**

Lord God, you lift the lowly high, you preserve and protect us on the day of trouble, and your steadfast love endures forever. **R**

Holy Spirit, transform us by the renewal of our minds, that we may be able to both discern and do your will, for this is true spiritual worship. **R**

Holy Spirit, giver of gifts, source of our inspiration, we thank you for using our minds, hands, prayers and love as holy service. **R**

Lord Jesus Christ, when you ask us the question "Who do you say that I am"?, give us the boldness of Peter to confess you as "Messiah, the Son of the living God," that together we might help build your church in this place. **R**

We remember all the saints before us who have lived the faith and died with the joyful expectation of seeing you face to face. Thank you for using them for our sake, and may we serve others in like manner. **R**

You know the needs of the world, Lord Jesus Christ, before we recognize or name them. Yet you listen in joy as we bring before you those we know and often love more dearly than our own lives. Hear us as we pray for others: _____ . **R**

Your steadfast love is your daily gift for our daily need. Thank you, loving Lord. **Amen.**

Texts: Isaiah 51:1-6 or Exodus 1:8—2:10   Psalm 138 or Psalm 124   Romans 12:1-8   Matthew 16:13-20

Dates: August 21 – August 27

Time after Pentecost, Lectionary 22A

Responsive Sentence for the Sundays after Pentecost:
Prince of Peace: **Come, Lord Jesus, come.**

Heavenly Father, even as Jeremiah and Jesus suffered on account of your Holy Word, give us courage to speak in love what is precious in your sight. **R**

Lord God, Holy Spirit, you test our hearts and minds, but because your love is steadfast, may we always be able to sing songs of thanksgiving to you. **R**

Increase our zeal, Lord Jesus Christ, that we may we rejoice in hope, be patient in suffering, persevere in prayer, give generously and care for the visitor and stranger in our day. **R**

Keep us, Holy Spirit, from taking revenge upon those who wrong us, and help us learn how to overcome evil with good. **R**

Lord Jesus, when we pretend to know more than you, and what is best for ourselves and others, remind us of the cross you bore to do the Father's will. Give us courage to trust your will far above our own. **R**

Spirit of God, as you once moved over the face of this earth as Creator God, so teach us how to be caretakers of all that you have entrusted into our hands. **R**

We bring before you those with special needs. Remember, also, those who bring these names before you in faith that you will hear our prayers: _____. **R**

Your steadfast love is your daily gift for our daily need. Thank you, loving Lord. **Amen.**

Texts: Jeremiah 15:15-21 or Exodus 3:1-15   Psalm 26:1-8 or Psalm 105:1-6, 23-26, 45b   Romans 12:9-21   Matthew 16:21-28

Dates: August 28 – September 3

YEAR A

Time after Pentecost, Lectionary 23A

Responsive Sentence for the Sundays after Pentecost:
    Prince of Peace: **Come, Lord Jesus, come.**

Lord God, you gave us your law to warn us of danger, to show us our wrong doing and to guide us toward yourself. Help us receive your law as a sign of your love, for you take no pleasure in the consequences of our wrong doing. **R**

Give us teachers of your way, Lord God, and the strength to follow you all the days of our lives. **R**

Help us fulfill your law by loving our neighbor as we love ourselves. **R**

Lord Jesus, you promise to be with us every time we gather in your name. By your presence, even now, guide our ways and strengthen our faith. **R**

We bring before you all the institutions of mercy in every land. We thank you for all who serve, heal, pray and love the persons in their charge. **R**

Hear our prayers for those with special needs including the faithless, the atheists, the doubters, and the searchers for love and truth. Especially we ask you to be with those in physical, mental or spiritual need whom we name before you now: _____. **R**

Your steadfast love is your daily gift for our daily need. Thank you, loving Lord. **Amen.**

Texts: Ezekiel 33:7-11 or Exodus 12:1-14   Psalm 119:33-40 or Psalm 149   Romans 13:8-14   Matthew 18:15-20

Dates: September 4 – September 10

Time after Pentecost, Lectionary 24A

Responsive Sentence for the Sundays after Pentecost:
    Prince of Peace: **Come, Lord Jesus, come.**

Heavenly Father, we marvel with Joseph that you can bring good out of intended harm. Help us see your presence and purpose in all that comes upon us. **R**

Holy Spirit, remind us of God's benefits: the forgiving of our sins, the rescuing of our souls from the Pit, and your ever present steadfast love. **R**

Lord Jesus Christ, since we all belong to you, keep us from shunning one another when we quarrel over matters of faith and practice, for you love us all, and desire that we love one another. **R**

Lord Jesus Christ, forgiver of our every wrong, give us the power to forgive one another, painful as it may be. Help us also to forgive ourselves, that your death on the cross for our sin may not be in vain. **R**

We pray, Lord God, for the poor, for the weak in faith, and for those whose labors often seem to be in vain. Give us the eye to see beyond the boundary of this world, to hear your thank-you for honest labor, and to trust that you take note of all we try to give to you. **R**

We bring before you, in humble hope, all whom we name before you, believing that you are the healer of our many ills: _____. **R**

Your steadfast love is your daily gift for our daily need. Thank you, loving Lord. **Amen.**

Texts: Genesis 50:15-21 or Exodus 14:19-31   Psalm 103:[1-7] 8-13 or Psalm 114 or Exodus 15:1b-11, 20-21   Romans 14:1-12   Matthew 18:21-35

Dates: September 11 – September 17

Time after Pentecost, Lectionary 25A

Responsive Sentence for the Sundays after Pentecost:
  Prince of Peace: **Come, Lord Jesus, come.**

Gracious God, merciful One, slow to anger and abounding in steadfast love, thank you for sparing even the most evil, by sending yet another messenger to them with love and grace and a call to repentance. **R**

We praise you, Heavenly Father, for your goodness is abundant, your mighty works are gracious, and every generation of believers is your pride and joy. **R**

Lord Jesus Christ, you give us the privilege to believe in you and to suffer for you. Make us fear death as little as our nighttime sleep, for whether we live or die, you are by our side. **R**

Lord Jesus Christ, you are the vine and we are your branches. With glad hearts teach us not to worry about your harvest, but be mindful only of our faithful growing. **R**

Holy Spirit, encourage us to bring before you those with special needs for healing, believing that you care about each and every soul we name: _____. **R**

Your steadfast love is your daily gift for our daily need. Thank you, loving Lord. **Amen.**

Texts: Jonah 3:10—4:11 or Exodus 16:2-15   Psalm 145:1-8 or Psalm 105:1-6, 37-45   Philippians 1:21-30   Matthew 20:1-16

Dates: September 18 – September 24

Time after Pentecost, Lectionary 26A

Responsive Sentence for the Sundays after Pentecost:
    Prince of Peace: **Come, Lord Jesus, come.**

Heavenly Father, through your prophet Ezekiel, you have ordered us to cast away our transgressions, repent, and to receive from you a new heart and a new spirit. Help us to turn and live your way. **R**

Make known to us your ways, O Lord, bring us to repentance, and forget the sins of our past. **R**

Holy Spirit, help us to be of the same mind as Jesus Christ, to have the same love, and to do nothing selfish. **R**

Lord Jesus Christ, we bend our knees, hearts and minds when we hear the sound of your exalted name, and confess that you are our Lord. **R**

Jesus, Our Lord, may we recognize your authority over us, bend our wills to your desires, and believe with all our hearts that we can only change our lives through the power of the Holy Spirit. **R**

Holy God, as the nations of the world rise and fall before you, help us see your interventions into the affairs of humankind as interruptions of the loving Father, saving us from disaster. **R**

For those among us in need of our prayer for health and healing, be now the Great Physician, Lord Jesus, by serving those whom we now name aloud: _____. **R**

Your steadfast love is your daily gift for our daily need. Thank you, loving Lord. **Amen.**

Texts: Ezekiel 18:1-4, 25-32 or Exodus 17:1-7   Psalm 25:1-9 or Psalm 78:1-4, 12-16   Philippians 2:1-13 Matthew 21:23-32

Dates: September 25 – October 1

YEAR A

Time after Pentecost, Lectionary 27A

Responsive Sentence for the Sundays after Pentecost:
    Prince of Peace: **Come, Lord Jesus, come.**

As your vineyard, O Lord, help us be your pleasant planting as we exercise your justice and your righteousness in the world. **R**

Heavenly Father, protect your church from self-ruin, for you have planted us, nurtured us, and have shone the face of Christ upon us, that we may be saved. **R**

Lord Jesus Christ, to follow you is to gain everything, to know you is to know divine love, and to suffer for you is high honor. Help us know the power of your resurrection and be fearless in the hour of death. **R**

Holy Spirit, point out the cornerstone to us, even Jesus Christ the Lord, and give us the skill and the will to produce fruit fit for the kingdom of God. **R**

Let love, like rain, fall upon the just and the unjust. Open our eyes to the needs of people beyond our own family and church, that all your people in every land may taste and know that you are good. **R**

Lift up your healing arm, Lord God, and reach out to touch those among us who suffer from needs beyond our own ability to meet or cure: _____. **R**

Your steadfast love is your daily gift for our daily need. Thank you, loving Lord. **Amen.**

Texts: Isaiah 5:1-7 or Exodus 20:1-4, 7-9, 12-20   Psalm 80:7-15 or Psalm 19   Philippians 3:4b-14
Matthew 21:33-46

Dates: October 2 – October 8

Time after Pentecost, Lectionary 28A

Responsive Sentence for the Sundays after Pentecost:
Prince of Peace: **Come, Lord Jesus, come.**

Heavenly Father, thank you for fulfilling Isaiah's prophesy. You swallow up death forever, and wipe away the tears from all faces through the death and resurrection of our Lord Jesus Christ. **R**

Lord Jesus Christ, our Good Shepherd, restore our souls as we plan to live with you in the house of the Lord forever. **R**

Holy Spirit, we rejoice in the assurance that the Lord is near and that we have no need to worry about anything. Guard our hearts with the peace of Christ which passes all understanding. **R**

Lord Jesus Christ, you have called us to be your chosen people. Robe us in your garment of righteousness, that we may be included with all your saints of light. **R**

We thank you that we can envision those who have served you here on earth before us, and we are grateful that they are still useful to you in ways we can only imagine. **R**

Though the earth is filled with your glory, we also know that the earth is filled with suffering and sorrow. Lighten the burden of those who grieve with the promise of the Great Reunion, and touch the lives of those among us who suffer from all sorts of disease and pain: _____. **R**

Your steadfast love is your daily gift for our daily need. Thank you, loving Lord. **Amen.**

Texts: Isaiah 25:1-9 or Exodus 32:1-14   Psalm 23 or Psalm 106:1-6, 19-23   Philippians 4:1-9   Matthew 22:1-14

Dates: October 9 – October 15

YEAR A

Time after Pentecost, Lectionary 29A

Responsive Sentence for the Sundays after Pentecost:
  Prince of Peace: **Come, Lord Jesus, come.**

Holy Lord, Creator of light and darkness, joy and woe, we call you by name for there is no other god. **R**

Holy Spirit, hear us as we sing a new song to you, the only Lord of all the earth. We worship you in joy and trembling, so great is your name. **R**

Lord Jesus, help us believe that we have been chosen by you. Fill us with joy and conviction, as we wait for your return and your rescue from all that would do us harm. **R**

Lord Jesus Christ, you show no partiality among us by loving us all, as we are, where we are. In gratitude, help us give to God the things that are God's. **R**

Spare us all, Heavenly Father, from the ravages of nature, and teach us to how to prepare and protect one another from the storms of devastation. **R**

Lord Jesus, Great Physician, visit our sick, touch our untouchables, receive into your kingdom those who are ready to pass into your eternal care, and heal those for whom health may return: _____. **R**

Your steadfast love is your daily gift for our daily need. Thank you, loving Lord. **Amen.**

Texts: Isaiah 45:1-7 or Exodus 33:12-23   Psalm 96:1-9 [10-13] or Psalm 99   1 Thessalonians 1:1-10   Matthew 22:15-22

Dates: October 16 – October 22

Time after Pentecost, Lectionary 30A

Responsive Sentence for the Sundays after Pentecost:
    Prince of Peace: **Come, Lord Jesus, come.**

Heavenly Father, help us heed your teaching to seek justice for all, making no distinction between rich or poor, great or small, but to love our neighbor as we love ourselves. **R**

Holy Spirit, keep us on the path you lay before us, and teach us to regard the wicked as chaff which your Spirit will drive away. **R**

Holy Spirit, when opposition to the proclaiming of the gospel occurs, and our hearts are tested, keep us gentle in spirit, tenderly nursing those children of yours yet to know your mighty love. **R**

Holy God, we know we cannot be anything but indebted to you for all your kindness and mercies. Help us respond in love toward you and our neighbor. **R**

Holy Spirit, when our questions about God are used to excuse us from the faith, thwart our cleverness with questions of your own for us to answer. **R**

Lord Jesus Christ, healer of our many ills, look upon your church gathered at this hour in all places, and send your Holy Spirit with the gift of healing, even as we name those known to us who are in need: _____. **R**

Your steadfast love is your daily gift for our daily need. Thank you, loving Lord. **Amen.**

Texts: Leviticus 19:1-2, 15-18 or Deuteronomy 34:1-12   Psalm 1 or Psalm 90:1-6, 13-17   1 Thessalonians 2:1-8   Matthew 22:34-46

Dates: October 23 – October 29

Reformation Sunday

Responsive Sentence for Reformation Sunday:
   We hear God's holy invitation: **"Be still and know that I am God."**

Heavenly Father, forgiver of our every sin, in Christ we are your new people. Your law is written on our minds and hearts. Your gospel is in the marrow of our bones. Our souls exalt with the good news of your new covenant with us. **R**

Lord God, our refuge and strength, your wondrous works make wars cease, plots fail, evil kingdoms totter. **R**

Lord Jesus Christ, through your work of atonement for us, the righteousness of God has been disclosed apart from the law. We dare not boast except in your loving and sacrificial death for our salvation. **R**

Holy Spirit, inspire us with the truth that makes us free from fear, free from eternal death, free to be your disciples of grace, love, joy, peace and patience. **R**

In the noise of our clamoring cities and factories, in the loud debates of opinion and politics, reform us by quieting all fears and doubts as we listen for you. **R**

Christ our King, weeping over Jerusalem, praying for us to Our Father, promising a crucified thief paradise, providing family beneath the cross for Mary your mother, and for John your disciple, we pray that you will care for us too. **R**

Hear our gratitude for hospitals, laboratories, institutions of learning; for nurses and doctors and family members who attend to our needs, and for churches like this gathering, where we boldly name the names of those who need your healing touch: _____. **R**

Reform us, make us your saints in this church militant, and in the life to come, make us your saints in the church triumphant. Be our one and only King. **Amen**.

Texts: Jeremiah 31:31-34   Psalm 46   Romans 3:19-28   John 8:31-36

All Saints Sunday

Responsive Sentence for All Saints Sunday:
　　We hear God's holy invitation: **"Be still and know that I am God."**

Lord God Almighty, help us join in the vision of John and to sing with the multitude of believers, "Blessing and glory and wisdom and thanksgiving and honor and power and might be to our God forever and ever! Amen." **R**

Holy Spirit, with the Psalmist, let us bless your name, boast of your gospel, and say to our fears: "Be gone." **R**

Lord Jesus Christ, you elevate our station in life to be children of God. So let us trust you with all that we are, have and may become, trusting in your goodness. **R**

Lord Jesus, include us among the blessed as we mourn, for we are your people of hope and expectation. As we trust the power of gentleness, and as we hunger and thirst for righteousness, we know that these are God-given gifts of love. **R**

Lord Jesus, as we learn to will all things your way, purify our hearts. Make us your peacemakers, and when we suffer for the faith, grant us the ability to rejoice and be glad. **R**

For all the saints, living on earth or in the hereafter, we rejoice in your power to heal, inspire and resurrect. Hear us as we name those whom you have placed in our lives to love, both in this world and the next: _____. **R**

Reform us, make us your saints in this church militant, and in the life to come, make us your saints in the church triumphant. Be our one and only King. **Amen**.

Texts:　Revelation 7:9-17　Psalm 34:1-10, 22　1 John 3:1-3　Matthew 5:1-12

Time after Pentecost, Lectionary 31A

Responsive Sentence for the Sundays after Pentecost:
   Prince of Peace: **Come, Lord Jesus, come.**

Heavenly Father, keep us from living in false hope. Raise up the voice of the true prophet, and open the eye of your seer. You have sent us your Son, the Light of the World, that we may not have to live in the dark. **R**

Holy Spirit, keep us from having a disquieted soul and help us release the joy we have within, with song, prayer, and praise. **R**

Father God, deal with us as no earthly father is able, with a never-failing love, as an ever-present guide, and as healer of our every need. **R**

Lord Jesus, when you humble us, do so to keep us from being too proud, too in love with this world, too blinded to the needs of others. **R**

Holy God, Creator of worlds beyond this earth, yet willing to be born here, die here and rise here, give us a vision of your great love that is not confined to any place, any planet, or any solar system, for you have made much more. **R**

Lord Jesus, when we think that our needs are too small to bring before you, remind us of your invitation to ask, receive, and know healing. Great God, we now name people in need, knowing that no need is too small for a great God like you: _____. **R**

Your steadfast love is your daily gift for our daily need. Thank you, loving Lord. **Amen.**

Texts: Micah 3:5-12 or Joshua 3:7-17   Psalm 43 or Psalm 107:1-7, 33-37   1 Thessalonians 2:9-13   Matthew 23:1-12

Dates: October 30 – November 5

Time after Pentecost, Lectionary 32A

Responsive Sentence for the Sundays after Pentecost:
   Prince of Peace: **Come, Lord Jesus, come.**

Holy Spirit, help us seek your salvation for you are our help and our deliverer. **R**

Heavenly Father, help us understand that the day of the Lord is the time when justice rolls down like water, and righteousness like an ever-flowing stream. **R**

Lord Jesus Christ, first to rise from the dead, never to die again, keep us from grieving like those who have no hope. Fill us with the expectation of an eternal reunion with all we have loved and lost. **R**

Make us wise, Holy Spirit, like bridesmaids prepared for a longer wait than expected. When you come, at an hour no one knows, make us ready to receive you in joy. **R**

All the earth groans in tribulation, Heavenly Father, and without your intervention, earth itself could be destroyed by war. Turn us always toward your Son, Jesus Christ, the peacemaker. **R**

Before you we bring the injured, the weary, the confused, and the ill, standing in the need of prayer. Hear us as we name them in our minds, from our hearts, and with our voices: _____. **R**

Your steadfast love is your daily gift for our daily need. Thank you, loving Lord. **Amen.**

Texts: Amos 5:18-24 or Wisdom of Solomon 6:12-16 or Joshua 24:1-3a, 14-25   Psalm 70 or Wisdom of Solomon 6:17-20 or Psalm 70   1 Thessalonians 4:13-18   Matthew 25:1-13

Dates: November 6 – November 12

YEAR A

Time after Pentecost, Lectionary 33A

Responsive Sentence for the Sundays after Pentecost:
    Prince of Peace: **Come, Lord Jesus, come.**

Heavenly Father, when the last great day of the earth comes, help us be ready for the end of all things, and for the beginning reign of your Son, our Lord, with deliverance in his hand. **R**

Dwell in our hearts, Holy Spirit, that we may count our days, and in so doing, gain a wise heart, fearing our return to the dust as little as a night-time sleep. **R**

Heavenly Father, the times and seasons of life are known only by you. Help us live the gospel that proclaims that we are destined not for wrath, but for salvation through our Lord Jesus Christ. **R**

Lord Jesus Christ, you warn us with your parables that God notes our everyday actions and judges the heart. Create in us a clean heart, O God. **R**

Lord Jesus Christ, we often live as though you are far away from us, taking no notice of our indifference to the needs of one another. Help us welcome you into our every moment of our every day. **R**

The cares of the world and the wrenching debates among us are ceaseless, and often devoid of your teachings or love. Make us remember all that you've taught us to be, by loving and caring for one another, both stranger and friend. Hear as we name those known to us who need you near: _____. **R**

Your steadfast love is your daily gift for our daily need. Thank you, loving Lord. **Amen.**

Texts: Zephaniah 1:7, 12-18 or Judges 4:1-7   Psalm 90:1-8 [9-11] 12 or Psalm 123   1 Thessalonians 5:1-11   Matthew 25:14-30

Dates: November 13 – November 19

Christ the King, Lectionary 34A

Responsive Sentence for Christ the King:
    We hear God's holy invitation: **"Be still and know that I am God."**

Lord God Almighty, shepherd us. Bring us back when we wander away from you. Feed us with the finest wheat, the Body of your Son, and let us lie down in the richest of pastureland, knowing that the care of the earth and of each of us on it is your joy and delight. **R**

Great King above all gods, hear our joyful song to the Rock of our Salvation, Jesus Christ. **R**

Holy Spirit, give us your spirit of wisdom as we come to know Christ the King. We anticipate the world to come as an eternal gift to us and the glorious inheritance for all the saints. **R**

Christ the King, on the day of resurrection and great joy, you will say "Come, inherit the kingdom." In that kingdom we shall see the hungry and thirsty who were fed and given drink, the strangers who were befriended, the poor who were clothed, the prisoners who were visited—all your children—all our brothers and sisters. **R**

Christ the King, when we are able to name the names of those in need, we are serving you. Hear us as we pray aloud for those you have placed in our lives to care for: _____. **R**

Reform us, make us your saints in this church militant, and in the life to come, make us your saints in the church triumphant. Be our one and only King. **Amen**.

Texts: Ezekiel 34:11-16, 20-24   Psalm 95:1-7a or Psalm 100   Ephesians 1:15-23   Matthew 25:31-46

Dates: November 20 – November 26

1st Sunday of Advent

Responsive Sentence for Advent
    Stir up your power and come: **Lord Jesus, live among us.**

O Lord, Our Father, you are our potter and we are your clay. Mold us and make us your living clay, that we may be of use to you. **R**

Let your face shine upon us, O Lord, that we may be a light for others to come to you in faith. **R**

You have called us, by grace, into the fellowship of your body, the church. Strengthen us with the spiritual gifts we need to live and share a faith worthy of your holy calling. **R**

Keep us awake, alert, and excited, Holy Spirit, for the day of Jesus' return. Gather us up to be your people, forever useful, forever blessed. **R**

The saints who have finished their course on earth still shine upon us like lights from above, when we gather to worship in your sanctuary. We thank you for their example, love, and inspiration. We expect to be with them again. **R**

We pray for the world in which you are born, that all among us who are poor, suffer injustice, live with war, and die in anguish, may see you as the true Hope of this world and the next. **R**

We bring before you all who suffer from loneliness, bewilderment, doubt, and despair. Hear our prayers for those in any physical need: _____. **R**

Let your light shine upon us and we shall be saved. **Amen.**

Texts: Isaiah 64:1-9   Psalm 80:1-7, 17-19   1 Corinthians 1:3-9   Mark 13:24-37

YEAR B

2nd Sunday of Advent

Responsive Sentence for Advent
    Stir up your power and come: **Lord Jesus, live among us.**

Heavenly Father, give us ears to hear your words of comfort from your prophet Isaiah. Prepare a path in the wilderness of our hearts for your Son's arrival. **R**

Righteous God and Prince of Peace, you blot out our sins and prepare a pathway in our hearts to see what the Psalmist sees: righteousness and peace have kissed each other; love and faithfulness have met. Pure joy. **R**

God of patience, as you wait for us to fully turn toward you with heart, mind and soul, fill us with patience for your promised return. Remind us that a thousand years are like one day for you. **R**

Lord Jesus Christ, the womb was not too dark for you, and a painful birth was not beneath your dignity. As the world waits for deliverance from evil, give our hearts a new birth so that we may willingly feel the pain of others, and seek to relieve it. **R**

Lord Jesus Christ, your advent is near. Help us repent and prepare, for the new day that is coming is brighter than ten thousand suns. **R**

We remember the needs of all who need assistance, care, love and the presence of another as friend. As we name those known to us with special needs, grant them mercy and healing: _____. **R**

Let your light shine upon us and we shall be saved. **Amen.**

Texts: Isaiah 40:1-11   Psalm 85:1-2, 8-13   2 Peter 3:8-15a   Mark 1:1-8

3rd Sunday of Advent

Responsive Sentence for Advent
    Stir up your power and come: **Lord Jesus, live among us.**

Heavenly Father, even as you created and tended the Garden of Eden, tend us like your fruitful plants, causing righteousness and praise to blossom among us and all nations. **R**

Help us exult with the Psalmist: "You have done great things for us." As you wipe away all tears of sadness from all of our eyes, make us rejoice without ceasing. Hear our happy laughter and our joyful songs in praise of your ever present love. **R**

Jesus Christ, light of the world, we are not worthy to touch your sandals, yet you bid us come into your open arms. **R**

Send us, Holy Spirit, even as John the Baptist was sent to proclaim the Lord's coming, and make us open to his arrival in our churches, our homes and especially within ourselves. **R**

As we prepare to celebrate your coming, help us go into all the world announcing this good news, with words, deeds of kindness, forgiveness of one another, and hope for tomorrow. **R**

We name those among us whom we know need help, intervention, healing and hope. Be with them, as we name their names before your altar of thanksgiving: _____. **R**

Let your light shine upon us and we shall be saved. **Amen.**

Texts: Isaiah 61:1-4, 8-11   Psalm 126 or Luke 1:46b-55   1 Thessalonians 5:16-24   John 1:6-8, 19-28

4th Sunday of Advent

Responsive Sentence for Advent
    Stir up your power and come: **Lord Jesus, live among us.**

Lord God Almighty, you are always on the move so that we may always know your presence. Wherever and everywhere we are, you are there among us. **R**

Come, Merciful Lord, with your aid. Fill us with the knowledge of your greatness, especially among your lowly servants. **R**

Holy Spirit, wise and eternal God, give us an obedient faith, trusting your Word every day of our lives. **R**

Holy Spirit, make us fearless servants, like Mary, knowing that nothing is impossible with God. Like Mary, we dare respond, "Here we are. Let it be according to your Word." **R**

Throughout the earth you come and are coming, forever incarnate, forever loving. Forget no nation, no tribe, no family, no single person on earth, but be our Comforter and Redeemer. **R**

The bodies we use in this world need healing every hour, even when we do not sense the problems within. Until we are given new bodies, fit for living in the world to come, hear our prayers for those with special need: _____. **R**

Let your light shine upon us and we shall be saved. **Amen.**

Texts: 2 Samuel 7:1-11, 16   Luke 1:46b-55 or Psalm 89:1-4, 19-26   Romans 16:25-27   Luke 1:26-38

Nativity of Our Lord
Christmas Eve, December 24th

Responsive Sentence for Christmas
    Once born in Bethlehem: **Be born in us today.**

We proclaim with the Psalmist: "The Lord is king! The world is firmly established; it shall never be moved. He will judge the peoples with equity." **R**

Let the heavens be glad, and let the earth rejoice, for the Lord is coming tonight. **R**

Unto us a child is given, and He is named Wonderful Counselor, Mighty God, Everlasting Father, Prince of Peace. **R**

In these days help us hear the angel's message: "Do not be afraid, the news is good, for this is the day of Messiah's birth. **R**

Hear our songs this night as we join in the chorus of the Heavenly Hosts, praising God and singing, "Glory to God in the highest, and peace to God's people on earth!" **R**

Thank you Father God, for your Son. Thank you, Holy Spirit, for calling us to belief. Thank you, Lord Jesus Christ, for coming to do your Godly work on earth for us. **R**

Let your light shine upon us and we shall be saved. **Amen.**

Texts: Isaiah 9:2-7   Psalm 96   Titus 2:11-14   Luke 2:1-14 [15-20]

Nativity of Our Lord
Christmas Day, December 25th

Responsive Sentence for Christmas
　　Once born in Bethlehem:　　　　　　**Be born in us today.**

We rejoice, Heavenly Father, to see salvation come in the form of your beloved Son, Jesus Christ. **R**

Holy Spirit, help us see the Light of the World dawning upon the earth, and hear our holy songs of joy. **R**

Merciful Lord, you come to us out of love, that we might become heirs expecting eternal life—pure gift of grace. **R**

Jesus Christ, Light of Light, very God of very God, begotten, not made, come into our lives as Lord and Master. **R**

On this day of Christ's birth, Holy Spirit, open our hearts to receive the divine gifts, as well as to give other gifts as we are able. **R**

Remembering all who need your healing presence, touch those whom we name with the gift most necessary for them to receive this day: _____. **R**

Let your light shine upon us and we shall be saved. **Amen.**

Texts:　Isaiah 62:6-12　Psalm 97　Titus 3:4-7　Luke 2:[1-7] 8-20

72　　　　　　　　　　　　　　　　　　　　　　　　　　　　　　　YEAR B

1st Sunday after Christmas Day

Responsive Sentence for Christmas
    Once born in Bethlehem: **Be born in us today.**

Heavenly Father, we rejoice in knowing that you do not focus on our helplessness or sinfulness. Rather, you call us "a crown of beauty in your hand, a royal diadem." **R**

We praise you, Lord God, like the Psalmists of old. You have made all the earth to sing your praises, and in your own image you have formed us. **R**

Lord God, in the fulness of time, you sent Jesus to us, born of a woman, that we might be your adopted children. Hear us as we acknowledge you as "Abba! Father!" **R**

Lord God, Simeon found peace when he looked upon Jesus, knowing that He was the promised Messiah. Give us Simeon's faith, his peace, and his courage to proclaim it aloud. **R**

Lord God, your prophet, Anna, saw in Jesus the very redemption of the world. Give us Anna's wisdom, her joy, her voice to proclaim it aloud. **R**

Great Physician, you bear the favor of God, and have powers to heal beyond our understanding. Hear the names of those we know who need you very near: _____. **R**

Let your light shine upon us and we shall be saved. **Amen.**

Texts: Isaiah 61:10—62:3   Psalm 148   Galatians 4:4-7   Luke 2:22-40

YEAR B

2nd Sunday after Christmas Day

Responsive Sentence for Christmas:
    Once born in Bethlehem: **Be born in us today.**

Almighty God, you comfort us and turn our mourning into joy when you guide us back into your presence. Help us "be radiant with the goodness of the LORD." **R**

Holy Spirit, bless our children, grant us peace, give favorable weather and water to all, and help us love your most holy word. **R**

Heavenly Father, you chose us before the foundation of the world to be blessed in Christ with the spirituality of love. As you have adopted us, help us revel in your care, your gifts, your holy will, and your plan for our eternal inheritance. **R**

Lord Jesus Christ, so close to the Heavenly Father's heart, give us the gift to believe that you have made us "children of God." **R**

Be born anew in us, Lord Jesus, that your Holy Spirit may be as real to us as our own breath, our own beating heart, our own sense of the Divine. **R**

We remember to bring before you all the saints who suffer for the faith, and all in any sort of need. Hear us as we recall them by name: _____. **R**

Let your light shine upon us and we shall be saved. **Amen.**

Texts: Jeremiah 31:7-14 or Sirach 24:1-12   Psalm 147:12-20 or Wisdom of Solomon 10:15-21   Ephesians 1:3-14
John 1:[1-9] 10-18

The Epiphany of Our Lord
January 6th

Responsive Sentence for the Epiphany of Our Lord:
Arise, shine, for the light has come: **The glory of the LORD has risen upon us.**

Heavenly Father, through your prophet Isaiah you have promised a great light that will draw all the nations to you. Help us see your presence in our time that we may radiate your joy in our own lives. **R**

Lord Jesus Christ, you defend the cause of the poor, and deliver the needy and those who have no helper. Use us as your heart, hands and feet to care for our poorer sisters and brothers, whose lives are as precious to you as our own. You make us see all your children as our own kin. **R**

We thank you, Lord Jesus Christ, for Paul, a prisoner for your sake. From him we learn that we are fellow heirs of the mystery, and members of the same body, sharing in you the promise of the gospel's great news. Make us servants of your grace, that your boundless riches may be known to all. **R**

Lord Jesus, born in Bethlehem, you were visited by star-following wise men from the East who wanted to see you face to face. Give us this same desire to see you, for you alone are due our homage. **R**

Holy Spirit, guide us like you guided the wise men from the East. When we come into the presence of the Lord, fill us with generosity to give gifts worthy of God's great mystery revealed through Him. **R**

We remember all who have special needs—the poor, the lonely, the distraught, those who sense no love, and those who need your healing presence. Hear us as we name them in our hearts or aloud: _____ . **R**

Make all our petitions selfless, like those you taught us to pray. **Amen.**

Texts: Isaiah 60:1-6   Psalm 72:1-7, 10-14   Ephesians 3:1-12   Matthew 2:1-12

YEAR B

Baptism of Our Lord
1st Sunday after Epiphany

Responsive Sentence for the Sundays after Epiphany:
  Let us walk: **In the light of the Lord.**

Heavenly Father, light-bringer to the world on the first day of creation and light-bearer of the world on the day of Jesus' incarnation, dispel all darkness from our lives by your mighty presence. **R**

Holy Spirit, come upon us like you came upon the disciples, that we may believe in Jesus as the Lord of our lives. **R**

Lord Jesus Christ, your Holy Spirit permeates the lives of your saints. Fill us with that same Spirit that we may be your faithful disciples. **R**

We thank you, Lord God, for our given names, spoken on the day of our baptism. We rejoice that our family name is "Christian." **R**

We remember the year gone by as yet another gift from you. Thank you for every healing, every person and every day you have granted, knowing that the best is yet to come. **R**

As this year unfolds with both hope and fear, help each of us see you in the faces of all who are in need, both physically and spiritually. Bless us as we seek to be a blessing to others. **R**

Jesus, Healer of our every need, we bring before you those known to us who need prayer, healing, and hope. We name each of them out of love: _____. **R**

Light of the world, shine upon us. **Amen.**

Texts: Genesis 1:1-5   Psalm 29   Acts 19:1-7   Mark 1:4-11

2nd Sunday after Epiphany

Responsive Sentence for the Sundays after Epiphany:
    Let us walk: **In the light of the Lord.**

Heavenly Father, help us be like the young child Samuel, open to hear your call and to be your servant. **R**

With the Psalmist we pray, "You knit me together in my mother's womb." You search us and know us, O Lord, all day, every day, in every way. You marvelously prepare us for the days of our lives, beyond what we can ever know or imagine. **R**

Holy Spirit, remind us that we have been bought with a price, and that you view each of us as a temple worthy of your habitation. Dwell in us and be our God. **R**

Lord Jesus Christ, as you called the disciples to follow you, give us ears to hear your voice, eyes to see you working among us, and a heart open for loving. **R**

Holy Spirit, help us be the peaceful heart and hands of Jesus in this conflicted world. **R**

Continue, Lord Jesus Christ, to attend to the people among us who are suffering physically and spiritually: _____. **R**

Light of the world, shine upon us. **Amen.**

Texts: 1 Samuel 3:1-10 [11-20]   Psalm 139:1-6, 13-18   1 Corinthians 6:12-20   John 1:43-51

3rd Sunday after Epiphany

Responsive Sentence for the Sundays after Epiphany:
   Let us walk: **In the light of the Lord.**

Lord God, we thank you for using reluctant Jonah to bring Nineveh to repentance. As you work through imperfect prophets, priests, pastors and laypersons to speak your Word, give us confidence that your powerful voice will be heard despite our weaknesses. **R**

Heavenly Father, you are steadfast love incarnate in Jesus Christ. As we seek to know you better, help us put our trust and our hearts into your tender care. **R**

Lord Jesus Christ, by your coming to earth as the babe in the manger, God has inserted Himself into the affairs of humanity. Give us a heart to praise your coming, and to believe that your resurrection is the promise of eternal life. **R**

Lord Jesus Christ, you proclaimed the good news of God's nearness. Turn us around from the pursuit of this world to trust in God's intimate involvement in our lives. **R**

Holy Spirit, inspire us to improve our stewardship of all that has been placed into our care, including the earth, all peoples, and the proclamation of the gospel. **R**

The lives of the members of your church militant stand in constant need of prayer. Hear us as we name the living saints who need your healing word: _____. **R**

Light of the world, shine upon us. **Amen.**

Texts: Jonah 3:1-5, 10   Psalm 62:5-12   1 Corinthians 7:29-31   Mark 1:14-20

4th Sunday after Epiphany

Responsive Sentence for the Sundays after Epiphany:
   Let us walk: **In the light of the Lord.**

Lord God Almighty, throughout history you have sought to reach us through covenants, prophets, steadfast love and the birth of the Savior, Jesus Christ. Help us believe in your never-ending quest to be the love of our lives. **R**

God of majesty and splendor, you never let go of any of us, rich or poor, healthy or ill, young or old. We thank you for your compassion. **R**

Help us, Holy Spirit, to consider how our life styles affect others in the faith, for good or for evil. Keep us from engaging in behavior that would cause another soul to sin. **R**

Lord Jesus Christ, you speak with such august authority that even evil spirits obey your commands. Help us always obey your Word with joy. **R**

Nations and leaders, causes and concerns, all come before your review for judgment. Only you can rightly discern the heart and soul of all we call good or evil in this world. **R**

Those among us who suffer from disease, misfortune, and wrongs are brought before you by name, that you may bring confidence to all that you are standing by their side: _____. **R**

Light of the world, shine upon us. **Amen.**

Texts: Deuteronomy 18:15-20   Psalm 111   1 Corinthians 8:1-13   Mark 1:21-28

YEAR B

5th Sunday after Epiphany

Responsive Sentence for the Sundays after Epiphany:
　　Let us walk:　　　　　　　　　　**In the light of the Lord.**

Almighty, Everlasting God, you never grow weary or faint. You never fear a single mortal, ruler or sinner. All is known by you and all are accountable to you. Give power to those among us who are weary, discouraged or confused. You are our hope and consolation. **R**

Heavenly Father, look upon the brokenhearted. Where hope is gone, where love is lost, bring a song of thanksgiving that a new day is coming, when all will be renewed and restored. **R**

For the sake of the gospel, help us share in the plight of all with special needs, that your will may be done, that justice may prevail, and that divine love may be known by all. **R**

The hard work of healing others, casting out demons, and facing death causes you to pray to Our Father. Help us emulate you in prayer when we are weary with well-doing. **R**

Lord Jesus Christ, you fearlessly face our enemies of sin, death and the devil. Hear our thanksgiving for taking on those over whom we are most powerless and afraid. We thank you for your intervention. **R**

Though our span of life varies greatly from person to person, we know that your time is not our time, and that all souls in your care are as precious as the most holy of saints. Hear us as we pray for others: _____. **R**

Light of the world, shine upon us. **Amen.**

Ttexts:　Isaiah 40:21-31　Psalm 147:1-11, 20c　1 Corinthians 9:16-23　Mark 1:29-39

6th Sunday after Epiphany

Responsive Sentence for the Sundays after Epiphany:
    Let us walk: **In the light of the Lord.**

Heavenly Father, even as you healed Naaman of both his leprosy and his pride, heal us of all that separates us from true health and from you. **R**

Lord God, no matter our feelings, our station in life, our wealth, health or lack thereof, we are only as secure as your nearness. We praise you for wanting to be our only God. **R**

Holy Spirit, help us care for souls beyond our own. Keep evangelism from dying in our churches, for you yearn to grant eternal life to all. **R**

Lord Jesus Christ, look with mercy upon all of us in our needs, especially those needs which we are most reluctant to acknowledge. Heal us from pride, selfishness, lethargy for the gospel, bad temperament, and the many unnamed other sins that inhabit our being. **R**

Holy Spirit, as we live our lives on earth, prepare us for the life that is to come. Increase our faith, give us an ear to hear God's response to our prayers, and fill us with the joy of receiving yet another day full of grace. **R**

Those whom we name before you are already known by you, but we lift them up aloud, because you promise to hear us when we pray: _____. **R**

Light of the world, shine upon us. **Amen.**

Texts: 2 Kings 5:1-14   Psalm 30   1 Corinthians 9:24-27   Mark 1:40-45

7th Sunday after Epiphany

Responsive Sentence for the Sundays after Epiphany:
   Let us walk: **In the light of the Lord.**

Heavenly Father, you are forever doing a new thing. You make paths in the wilderness, you ride the rivers, and you cross the desert. Yet your heart belongs to the people whom you have formed for yourself, that we might declare your praise. Blot out our transgressions and remember our sins no more. **R**

Holy Spirit, you provide happiness to those who consider the poor to be a part of their extended family. Be gracious to us, O Lord, and love us when we don't even know we are being loveless. **R**

Faithful Lord, you are forever saying "Yes" through your promises. Put your seal upon us, and give us your Spirit as our heart's first installment of receptive love. Lord Jesus Christ, you proclaim that some among us "will not taste death until the kingdom of God has come with power." Change us now by your Holy Spirit. **R**

In this season of Epiphany, reveal yourself to us in the humanity of others who have greater needs than we can imagine. We know that all whom we help are no less than our brother or sister, and no less than a beloved child of God. **R**

We remember to pray by name for those whom you have brought into our lives to love. By the power of your love, reach into the hearts of those whom we name before you: _____. **R**

Light of the world, shine upon us. **Amen.**

Texts: Isaiah 43:18-25   Psalm 41   2 Corinthians 1:18-22   Mark 2:1-12

8th Sunday after Epiphany

Responsive Sentence for the Sundays after Epiphany:
    Let us walk: **In the light of the Lord.**

Heavenly Father, even as you used Hosea and his wife, Gomer, to illustrate your steadfast love, open our hearts to see the depth of the love you have for us, even when we are less than faithful. **R**

Lord God, slow to anger, like a patient parent with a rebellious child, help us love your undeserved compassion, and correct our wayward paths. **R**

Spirit of the living God, as you write your love for us on our hearts for others to read, and in our hearts to know that we are you own, move us to love others even as we are being loved. **R**

Lord Jesus, you call us to become your disciples as surely as you called other sinners to discipleship. Though none of us are worthy to call ourselves by your name, you use us as powerful witnesses to grace. **R**

We thank you, Holy Spirit, for every moment of grace that comes our way, even during this hour of worship with other grace-seekers. As you make this gathering of saints and sinners your church, hear our heartfelt thanksgiving for your call to serve. **R**

The problems of being in human form are well known by you, Great Physician. Attend to the needs of persons we know who worry, suffer, grieve, and long for a healthier life: _____. **R**

Light of the world, shine upon us. **Amen.**

Texts: Hosea 2:14-20   Psalm 103:1-13, 22   2 Corinthians 3:1-6   Mark 2:13-22

Transfiguration of Our Lord

Responsive Sentence for the Transfiguration of Our Lord:
    Lord of the Transfiguration: **Change us by your Word.**

Heavenly Father, working through human events to show your presence and strength, work through each of us as we seek to respond to your call to serve. **R**

Almighty God, shine in our lives like you do in the universe, maintaining life, order, balance and forever making new creations. Mend us as needed, bend us as necessary, that we may be your new creation, in body, mind and spirit. **R**

Holy Spirit, put your seal upon us that we may be filled with zeal for God's work through us as His agents of reconciliation. **R**

Lord Jesus Christ, when we do not know what to do when we are overwhelmed by God's intervention in our lives, give us the wisdom to listen, to marvel, and to renew our commitment to follow you all the days of our lives. **R**

Transfigure your world as you transfigure your church, Lord God, that all may be made new and whole. **R**

We pray for all who have needs beyond our power to meet, knowing that you, alone, are the Great Physician: _____. **R**

Light of the world, shine upon us. **Amen.**

Texts: 2 Kings 2:1-12   Psalm 50:1-6   2 Corinthians 4:3-6   Mark 9:2-9

Ash Wednesday

Responsive Sentence for Ash Wednesday:
    The day of the Lord is coming: **He abounds in steadfast love.**

Lord God Almighty, your prophets warn us to tremble at your coming, for it will be a day of darkness and gloom. They advise us to return to you with our hearts, so that our gloom may be turned into the noonday sun, for you are also gracious and merciful. **R**

Have mercy on us, O God, and blot out our sins. Against you and you alone have we sinned, for all our wrong against others is against a beloved child of your own. Create in us new hearts, and put a new and right spirit within us. **R**

Lord Jesus Christ, as fellow servants of God we may be treated as imposters, yet you make us true. We may be accused of being sorrowful, but we rejoice in your presence. We may be pitied because we are seen as poor and having nothing but faith, but you make us rich in the love of God. **R**

Holy Spirit, help us hear the words of Jesus as the Word of God. Help our hearts treasure your presence more than the treasures of the world. When we do find ourselves loving you above all else, help us to be humble in spirit, for it is your gift, not our accomplishment. **R**

We bring before you those who are well aware of their physical weaknesses, for they stand in need of your healing. As we name them aloud or silently in our hearts, help us remember again that we, too, are dust, and to dust we shall return: _____. **R**

Though we remember we are dust and to dust we shall return, we remember that we are your precious dust. **Amen.**

Texts: Joel 2:1-2, 12-17 or Isaiah 58:1-12   Psalm 51:1-17   2 Corinthians 5:20b—6:10   Matthew 6:1-6, 16-21

1st Sunday in Lent

Responsive Sentence for the Sundays in Lent:
    The day of the Lord is coming: **He abounds in steadfast love.**

Heavenly Father, Creator of all the creatures of the earth, with your rainbow in the sky you give a sign of your promise to protect all living beings from a worldwide flood. **R**

O LORD, God of our salvation, lead us in your truth, teach us your ways, forgive and forget our transgressions, and be generous with your loving mercy. **R**

Righteous Christ, suffering death for our sins, fill us with thanksgiving for your sacrifice, and with joy for our new life with you. **R**

Help us receive with faith the good news that the kingdom of God is near. **R**

Holy Spirit, help us insist on justice for all, even as we share our faith, our time, and are ever mindful of the needs of the poor. **R**

Healing Lord, hear our prayers for those among us who are ill, sad, confused or lonely. Make us ministers to each of them, even as we name them aloud: _____. **R**

Though we remember we are dust and to dust we shall return, we remember that we are your precious dust. **Amen.**

Texts: Genesis 9:8-17   Psalm 25:1-10   1 Peter 3:18-22   Mark 1:9-15

2nd Sunday in Lent

Responsive Sentence for the Sundays in Lent:
   The day of the Lord is coming: **He abounds in steadfast love.**

Creator of the nations, your bold covenant with Abraham and Sarah is still being kept. Help us walk before you, grateful to be recipients of your faithful promises. **R**

Lord God, you do not despise the laments of those in dire need. You promise that the poor shall eat and be satisfied, and the yet unborn will proclaim your mercy. **R**

Holy Spirit, you turn our hearts toward faith as the means by which we know we are your children. Keep us from wavering in our trust in Jesus, who was handed over to death for us, and raised for our justification. **R**

Lord Jesus Christ, like Peter, not knowing how formidable are our enemies, we would spare you and ourselves from suffering. Nevertheless, by your cross and passion you have defeated sin, death and the devil. **R**

Heavenly Father, you so loved the world that your gave your only Son. It is the singular gift beyond all others—your divine love for us. Hear our prayerful thank you. **R**

Suffering among us is always present, and we ask you to take care of those we name before you who have special needs for your presence and healing: _____. **R**

Though we remember we are dust and to dust we shall return, we remember that we are your precious dust. **Amen.**

Texts: Genesis 17:1-7, 15-16   Psalm 22:23-31   Romans 4:13-25   Mark 8:31-38 or Mark 9:2-9

YEAR B

3rd Sunday in Lent

Responsive Sentence for the Sundays in Lent:
    The day of the Lord is coming: **He abounds in steadfast love.**

Heavenly Father, help us receive and obey your commandments in the manner in which you gave them to us, out of perfect love and respect for one another. **R**

That which you have created praises you. May the glory of your heavens and the holiness of your commandments make the meditations of our hearts acceptable to you, O Lord, our Rock and our Redeemer. **R**

Lord God, Creator, Redeemer and Sanctifier, you thwart human logic with divine action, so that we may approach you by faith alone. **R**

Lord Jesus Christ, you are the very temple of God. Though our buildings of worship may return to the earth from which they were created, you live on in the hearts and lives of all your people. **R**

Bless the scientists who seek to discover your ways of creation, the healing powers of medicines, and the mysteries of all that you have created and still support. All is yours, and all goodness is from you. **R**

Crucified Lord and Savior, mend our broken lives with your healing touch. May those who feel the weight of this world's pains and woes, also know of your love and deliverance: _____. **R**

Though we remember we are dust and to dust we shall return, we remember that we are your precious dust. **Amen.**

Texts: Exodus 20:1-17   Psalm 19   1 Corinthians 1:18-25   John 2:13-22

4th Sunday in Lent

Responsive Sentence for the Sundays in Lent:
    The day of the Lord is coming: **He abounds in steadfast love.**

Heavenly Father, when we feel that we have lost direction as a people, or even as a person, help us remember your presence in our wilderness journeys. **R**

Great Deliverer, your steadfast love and wonderful works have spared us of troubles known and unknown, for you are in love with us. **R**

Holy Spirit, help us remember the great work that Christ accomplished for us, which no other person could perform. Help us confess with gladness, "by grace we have been saved." **R**

Lord Jesus Christ, gift of mercy from God the Father, you love us even when we are most unlovable, lost, and afraid. Thank you for your grace. **R**

Lord Jesus Christ, lifted up on the cross like the serpent in the wilderness, lift up our eyes to see you as the Lord and Savior, loving God's whole world. **R**

We bring before you those whom you love with special needs, known to us as family and friends: _____. **R**

Though we remember we are dust and to dust we shall return, we remember that we are your precious dust. **Amen**.

Texts: Numbers 21:4-9   Psalm 107:1-3, 17-22   Ephesians 2:1-10   John 3:14-21

5th Sunday in Lent

Responsive Sentence for the Sundays in Lent:
  The day of the Lord is coming: **He abounds in steadfast love.**

Lord God, forgiver of our every sin, remind us to forgive and forget the wrongs that have come upon us by others. Help us joyfully receive, and joyfully give grace for ourselves and for others. **R**

Holy Spirit, help us understand that all of our sin against another is mostly a sin against you. Wash us with your forgiving love, and we shall be whiter than snow. **R**

Teach us your laws, Lord God, and as we meditate upon your wisdom, help us follow your guidance and decrees. **R**

Lord Jesus Christ, even as you submitted to the will of Our Father, even unto death, help us give in willingly to your superior way. **R**

Lord Jesus Christ, like a grain of wheat in spring soil, so you have risen from the grave. Help us become your living fruit, by seeking your Lordship in all we do and say. **R**

Heavenly Father, even as Jesus' soul was troubled when death came near, draw us near to you in the hour of our dying, that we may be reunited with all the saints. **R**

Great Physician, reach out to those whom we name in need of help and healing: _____. **R**

Though we remember we are dust and to dust we shall return, we remember that we are your precious dust. **Amen.**

Texts: Jeremiah 31:31-34   Psalm 51:1-12   Hebrews 5:5-10   John 12:20-33

6th Sunday in Lent
Sunday of the Passion, Palm Sunday

Responsive Sentence for Palm Sunday:
　　Blessed is He who comes in the name of the Lord:　　**Hosanna in the highest!**

Lord Jesus Christ, you came into Jerusalem on a donkey, as God's humble peacemaker, not like a conquering king on horseback. **R**

Heavenly Father you sent the prophet Isaiah with the Word and with a heart full of love. **R**

Holy Spirit, you came to a persecuted and troubled Psalmist, who put his trust in you when he proclaimed, "You are my God, my times are in your hand." **R**

Lord Jesus Christ, you emptied yourself, taking the form of a slave, and being obedient unto death, even death on a cross. **R**

Lord Jesus Christ, you come even to us, with your passion, your suffering, your death-defeating love. You bid us, likewise, to bear one another's burdens. **R**

Come to those among us, and visit all with your compassion, love and healing: _____. **R**

Though we remember we are dust and to dust we shall return, we remember that we are your precious dust. **Amen.**

Texts for the Liturgy of the Palms:　　Mark 11:1-11 or John 12:12-16　　Psalm 118:1-2, 19-29

Texts for the Liturgy of the Passion:　　Isaiah 50:4-9a　　Psalm 31:9-16　　Philippians 2:5-11　　Mark 14:1—15:47 or Mark 15:1-39 [40-47]

YEAR B

Maundy Thursday

Responsive Sentence for Maundy Thursday:
  Let us love one another: **As Christ has loved us.**

Lord Jesus Christ, we often see Peter's reluctance to have you wash his feet as our hesitation in all things spiritual, for you end up touching the physical. You end up touching us. Give us the courage to let you touch us, head to toe. **R**

Lord Jesus Christ, you command us to wash each other's feet. The indignity never ends! Yet we know what to ask. Give us the courage to touch one another, for the sake of healing, head to toe. **R**

Holy Spirit, courage-giver, teach us how to bend our knees, fold our hands, and lift up our eyes to the loving Father, who cared so much that He sent us His Son to die for us. We cannot match the humiliation of Jesus, but we give thanks for His holy work on our behalf. **R**

Heavenly Father, you single us out for love of such depth and beauty that we can scarcely stand it, or understand it. For the love of us, you gave your only Son! **R**

Your new commandment, Lord Jesus, is to love one another as you have loved us. When you kneel before us, towel in hand, we know we are not worthy. Wash us anyway. Make us humble. Help us be each other's keeper. **R**

Though we remember we are dust and to dust we shall return, we remember that we are your precious dust. **Amen.**

Texts: Exodus 12:1-4 [5-10] 11-14   Psalm 116:1-2, 12-19   1 Corinthians 11:23-26   John 13:1-17, 31b-35

Good Friday

Responsive Sentence for Good Friday:
    God of the ages: **You love us.**

Heavenly Father, the pain of Good Friday is rebellion against you. You sent a Son, your one and only, and they crucified Him because all generations want a God unlike the God who is you. It is our sin to want you to be bold and brave, strong and militant, rather than a God filled with so much mercy and love. **R**

Holy Spirit, you were there in power, giving Jesus the will to die for the likes of us. We do not know what you whispered in His heart, or what you reminded Him of in His memory. We only know He did not stop the awful crucifixion, which was His alone to cancel. **R**

Lord Jesus Christ, we see ourselves in Pontius Pilate, your judge. He was trapped, like we are, dealing with you on this earth where justice so often means punishment. He did not know how to say "no" to death. **R**

Forgive us, Father, Son and Holy Spirit. We do not know all that we have done. It is not our ignorance which emboldens us to ask for forgiveness. It is your death, your love, your power and your mercy. And more than all of this, it is our desire to be with you forever. **R**

Into your hands we commend all who do not know you, but need you. Help us ache for their discovery of a God so good that He loves even those of us who walk away. **R**

Though we remember we are dust and to dust we shall return, we remember that we are your precious dust. **Amen.**

Texts: Isaiah 52:13—53:12   Psalm 22   Hebrews 10:16-25 or Hebrews 4:14-16; 5:7-9   John 18:1—19:42

YEAR B

Easter Day
Resurrection of Our Lord

Responsive Sentence for the Sundays of Easter:
    Set our minds on heavenly things: **Fill us with your joy.**

Lord Jesus Christ, we witness with Peter that you are the fulfillment of the prophets' testimony, the judge of the living and the dead, and the forgiver of our sin. As you defeated death by rising from the dead, fill us with the real expectation of life eternal. **R**

Heavenly Father, you wipe away all disgrace and all tears from our faces. You are the God for whom we have waited. We rejoice in your salvation in the sending of your Son. **R**

Give us ears to hear and a heart to believe the proclamation of the gospel, that we may be counted among your disciples. **R**

Lord Jesus, your disciples fled from the empty tomb in terror and amazement. Come, visit with us, that all our fears may dissipate in your presence. **R**

Lord Jesus Christ, help us see you as clearly as Mary Magdalene saw you standing at your grave site. Give us her courage to proclaim that you are alive, and still among us. **R**

Heal all of us Lord, from doubt, worry, loneliness and fearfulness. Tend to those among us with special needs: _____. **R**

Help us listen closely to your Word, even as you listen closely to our prayers. **Amen.**

Texts: Acts 10:34-43 or Isaiah 25:6-9   Psalm 118:1-2, 14-24   1 Corinthians 15:1-11 or Acts 10:34-43
John 20:1-18 or Mark 16:1-8

2nd Sunday of Easter

Responsive Sentence for the Sundays of Easter:
  Set our minds on heavenly things: **Fill us with your joy.**

Holy Spirit, help your fractured church to be of one heart and soul, that our proclamation will resonate with great power, and great grace may be upon us all. **R**

Lord Jesus Christ, you prayed to Our Father that we would be one church. Help us receive you like Aaron, rejoicing with precious oil upon his head. Help us receive you like morning dew upon the mountains, valleys and prairies. Help us rely upon your precious promise of life forevermore. **R**

Word of Life, eternal life, make our joy complete with the God of light, in whom there is no darkness at all. **R**

Heavenly Father, forgiver of our every sin, help us look to Jesus Christ, your beloved Son, as our advocate and redeemer, not only for ourselves, but for your whole world. **R**

Lord Jesus Christ, when we behave like Thomas, letting ourselves be filled with doubt, give us strength to constantly return to your church, with our doubt, until we confess "My Lord and My God." **R**

We bring before you people we know with special needs, burdens too heavy to bear alone, disease that will not be healed on this earth, and afflictions that can only be healed by your precious touch: _____. **R**

Help us listen closely to your Word, even as you listen closely to our prayers. **Amen.**

Texts: Acts 4:32-35   Psalm 133   1 John 1:1—2:2   John 20:19-31

YEAR B

3rd Sunday of Easter

Responsive Sentence for the Sundays of Easter:
	Set our minds on heavenly things: **Fill us with your joy.**

Lord Jesus Christ, Author of life, help us believe Peter's bold proclamation of your resurrection, of your healing presence, and that you are the suffering forgiver of our many sins. **R**

Heavenly Father, when we are in distress remind us of your Son, who makes room for us in this world and the next. **R**

Holy Spirit, help us love being a child of God, for there is no higher calling. **R**

When we are startled and terrified by your unexpected presence, Lord Jesus Christ, help us hear your word of peace. Touch us as we seek to touch you. **R**

Come to us Lord Jesus, be at our table. As you visited with your disciples after your resurrection, and ate with them, come, Lord Jesus, be our guest today. **R**

We name aloud those who are hungry for your touch, ready for your healing, or nearing the new life: _____. **R**

Help us listen closely to your Word, even as you listen closely to our prayers. **Amen.**

Texts: Acts 3:12-19   Psalm 4   1 John 3:1-7   Luke 24:36b-48

4th Sunday of Easter

Responsive Sentence for the Sundays of Easter:
Set our minds on heavenly things: **Fill us with your joy.**

Lord Jesus Christ, be the cornerstone of our lives, for there is no other name by which we may be saved. **R**

Holy Spirit, when we talk about God, help us begin to talk with God, for He is always with us. **R**

Heavenly Father, you show us your love by sending your only Son to die for us. Help us love one another by the willful laying down of our lives for others. **R**

Good Shepherd, Jesus Christ, you know your own. You also know the Heavenly Father like no other being, and you obey His commands. Give us the will to know you intimately, like no other, and to trust you with the living and the giving of our lives for others. **R**

Holy Spirit, you search us and you know us better than we know ourselves. When you answer our prayers in ways we cannot understand, help us understand that you know what is best for us. **R**

As we set our minds on heavenly things, Lord Jesus Christ, we name those among us in need of heavenly intervention and healing: _____. **R**

Help us listen closely to your Word, even as you listen closely to our prayers. **Amen.**

Texts: Acts 4:5-12   Psalm 23   1 John 3:16-24   John 10:11-18

YEAR B

5th Sunday of Easter

Responsive Sentence for the Sundays of Easter:
  Set our minds on heavenly things: **Fill us with your joy.**

Holy Spirit, give us the courage of Philip who took the time to share his faith with a curious stranger. **R**

Heavenly Father, we are the people that were yet unborn when the Psalmist in exultation exclaimed: "future generations will be told about the Lord." May we care about the yet unborn, and may our faith be as strong as the Psalmist's. **R**

Lord Jesus Christ, help us love one another, for when we do, we are loving you. **R**

Holy Spirit, we dare ask you to help us love more fervently, to love when love is hard to do, and to remember that when we love, it is only possible because you first loved us. **R**

Lord Jesus Christ, apart from you we can not bear fruit for the kingdom. Abide in us for the sake of your church, and help us be your love-filled disciples. **R**

Holy Spirit, when we see violence, help us also see the sadness of your heart, and seek to be your peacemakers in our everyday lives. **R**

Lord Jesus, healer of bodies and healer of souls, hear the names of those in need of your touch: _____. **R**

Help us listen closely to your Word, even as you listen closely to our prayers. **Amen.**

Texts: Acts 8:26-40   Psalm 22:25-31   1 John 4:7-21   John 15:1-8

6th Sunday of Easter

Responsive Sentence for the Sundays of Easter:
    Set our minds on heavenly things: **Fill us with your joy.**

Holy Spirit, when we lift Jesus up with thanksgiving and praise, it is your Spirit upon us that makes us glad in worship. **R**

Heavenly Father, you are immersed in our lives, far beyond our knowing, for your steadfast love and your intervention into the affairs of humankind continue. With lyre and trumpets, with the roaring sea and the clapping waters, hear our praise for your marvelous work among us. **R**

Lord Jesus Christ, we believe you are the Messiah. Help us love what you love, obey as you obeyed, and serve as you served, for it is faith active in love that conquers the world. **R**

Lord Jesus Christ, help us love with the great love. When we do great love, you are our most intimate friend. Choose us again. Appoint us for service, and give us the grace to say thank you for using us in your kingdom on earth. **R**

Heavenly Father, your all-seeing eye knows the hostilities that still thrive among nations, religions, and families. Help us see others as your friends, so that we may not be so quick to judge nor condemn. **R**

Healer of our every ill, among us are needs so great as to be untouchable by our own strength to solve or cure. Continue your miracles, reach out and heal, even as we pray the names known to us: _____. **R**

Help us listen closely to your Word, even as you listen closely to our prayers. **Amen.**

Texts: Acts 10:44-48   Psalm 98   1 John 5:1-6   John 15:9-17

7th Sunday of Easter

Responsive Sentence for the Sundays of Easter:
    Set our minds on heavenly things: **Fill us with your joy.**

Holy God, as we share in the ministry of Jesus Christ, forbid us from trying to direct Him, or the Father, or the Holy Spirit, away from your own holy will. **R**

Holy Spirit, give us the spirit of a Psalmist, who can look at the wicked as mere chaff which the wind drives away, for the Lord is watching over us. **R**

Lord Jesus Christ, it is nothing less than eternal life that you offer as your gift to the world. With our praise and our witness to your love, hear our eternal thank you. **R**

Lord Jesus Christ, when you pray for us we marvel. You ask the Father to protect us from the evil one, because you claim us as your own. Increase our devotion to your word, which is truth both on earth and in heaven. **R**

Heavenly Father, we pray for our enemies, and for all who know only the power of strength to prevail. Steady our hearts in the time of conflict and war, for your Son is the ultimate peacemaker. **R**

For the sake of rescue and healing, Lord Jesus Christ, we bring before you the names of friends and loved ones, who, like all of us, need prayer: _____. **R**

Help us listen closely to your Word, even as you listen closely to our prayers. **Amen.**

Texts: Acts 1:15-17, 21-26   Psalm 1   1 John 5:9-13   John 17:6-19

The Day of Pentecost

Responsive Sentence for the Day of Pentecost:
   Holy Spirit, loving God:　　　　　　**Fill us with your Spirit.**

Heavenly Father, God Almighty, when we call on your name, you pour out your Holy Spirit upon us, young and old, slave or free, granting dreams and visions and confidence in the saving grace of Jesus Christ, Our Lord. **R**

When we are dried out like bones in the desert, renew us with your Holy Spirit. **R**

Holy Spirit, renew the face of the earth, and renew the hearts of your people. **R**

Intercede for us, Holy Spirit, when our poor prayers seem lacking, and we do not know how to rightly form our thoughts. **R**

We hope for what we cannot see, Lord Jesus Christ. We expect your adoption of each of us, for we are the Heavenly Father's special creation. **R**

Lord Jesus Christ, you have sent us the loving Advocate, the Spirit of Truth, that we may hope beyond "wishful thinking" to "great expectations" of eternal life with you. **R**

Great Physician, you know that some among us are ready to die; others want desperately to live longer, and many need healing and relief from pain. Help us yield to your will, knowing that you care for each of us. Use each of us, and our sufferings, for purposes beyond our understanding. We name each other in love, and in expectation of your better will: _____. **R**

Come Holy Spirit, come with your life-giving care and joy. **Amen.**

Texts: Acts 2:1-21 or Ezekiel 37:1-14   Psalm 104:24-34, 35b   Romans 8:22-27 or Acts 2:1-21   John 15:26-27; 16:4b-15

The Holy Trinity
First Sunday after Pentecost

Responsive Sentence for the Holy Trinity:
Holy, holy, holy, Lord God of hosts: **The whole earth is full of your glory.**

Lord God of hosts, you are always asking, "Whom shall I send?" Give each of us the courage of Isaiah to respond, "Here am I, send me." **R**

You are beautiful, Lord God, because you are holy, and your voice is all powerful. Give strength to your people, and give the blessings of your peace. **R**

Spirit of God, when we are fearful you ask us, "Why? Are you not my adopted ones?" **R**

Lord Jesus Christ, you speak to us of heavenly things, even when we are most interested in earthly things. Speak to us in the night-times of our lives, that we may learn the Way and the Will of your Holy Spirit. **R**

The problems of the nations, the politics of parties, the threats and fears of peoples everywhere are all known to you, Almighty God. Save us from fear, greed, revenge, and all evil things that keep us away from love. **R**

The dying, the sick, the lonely and the forsaken are your special people, for you know the names of each, even as we call upon you, once again, to remember them: _____. **R**

Come Holy Spirit, come with your life-giving care and joy. **Amen.**

Texts: Isaiah 6:1-8   Psalm 29   Romans 8:12-17   John 3:1-17

Time after Pentecost, Lectionary 8B

Responsive Sentence for the Sundays after Pentecost:
    Loving God, you hear our prayers: **You live among us.**

God of the covenant, you made us the promise to be our God forever, even as Hosea promised loyalty to his spouse. Keep us faithful to you. **R**

Gracious and Merciful God, make us sing like a Psalmist, for you have compassion on us, your children. **R**

Holy Spirit, as you inspired Paul to paint a picture for us, not on a hard tablet of stone, but on the tablets of our own human hearts, help us see ourselves held within your divine heart—ever near, and ever dear. **R**

Lord Jesus Christ, help us hear you say to each one of us: "Follow me." And when we hear this calling, give us the courage to follow you. **R**

With the memory of your birth, the wise men at your manger, the revealing of yourself as God in flesh made manifest, your suffering at Calvary, and your resurrection from the dead, be with us as we journey through this Pentecost season, that we may be better disciples. **R**

Lord Jesus, look with compassion upon those among us struggling for wholeness and health. As we name their names, touch them, one by one: _____. **R**

The love of God has won. The new life has begun. **Amen.**

Texts: Hosea 2:14-20   Psalm 103:1-13, 22   2 Corinthians 3:1-6   Mark 2:13-22

Dates: May 24 – May 28

Time after Pentecost, Lectionary 9B

Responsive Sentence for the Sundays after Pentecost:
Loving God, you hear our prayers: **You live among us.**

Lord God Almighty, as we are gathered for worship to keep this sabbath day holy, remind us of the history of our salvation, that we may marvel at your love and obey all your commandments. **R**

Holy Spirit, lift our voices to sing and shout our joy for your rescue of us from meaninglessness, selfishness, and despair, for you are alive and among us. **R**

Lord Jesus, we know that death is at work in us, but we also believe that life is at work in us, through you and for all eternity. Help us claim the greater good. **R**

Soften the hardness of our hearts, Lord Jesus, and heal us of all that would wither without your constant strength and healing, including our bodies, our souls, our faiths, and our purposes for being. **R**

Lord of the Sabbath, Jesus Christ, you gave us this day for the re-creation of our spirits, and we give thanks for every holy word that we hear in worship. **R**

The newborn, the strong and the dying are all charges under your care, Lord God. Bless us and hear us as we speak the names of those we know who long for help and healing: _____. **R**

The love of God has won. The new life has begun. **Amen.**

Texts: Deuteronomy 5:12-15 or 1 Samuel 3:1-10 [11-20]   Psalm 81:1-10 or Psalm 139:1-6, 13-18
2 Corinthians 4:5-12   Mark 2:23—3:6

Dates: May 29 – June 4

Time after Pentecost, Lectionary 10B

Responsive Sentence for the Sundays after Pentecost:
    Loving God, you hear our prayers: **You live among us.**

Heavenly Father, you heard the excuses of Adam and Eve for their personal sins, even as you hear our own excuses, yet you do not forsake any of us. **R**

Give us the ears of Adam and Eve to hear you walking nearby, knowing our wrong. You never hide from us, though we may try to hide from you. **R**

Lord Jesus Christ, like our Scriptural ancestors, we often prefer an earthly king or queen, instead of your kindly rule. Forgive us, King of kings. **R**

Your steadfast love calls us back to your mercy. Hear our cries of remorse and taste our tears of longing, even as our sin causes us to seek for your forgiveness. **R**

Heavenly Father, even as you raised Jesus from the dead, each of us must come before you after we die. We shall not lose heart for that day or reckoning, for your grace is love, and you have promised us an eternal home. **R**

Lord God, creator of the universe, our very earth trembles and shakes. Storms destroy. Seas rise and tsunamis kill, yet all of science, history, and theology must yield to the mystery of your love for us, which saves, restores, renews and is forever. **R**

Illness, Lord God, for us, is so fearful. For you it is only a change in our situation, for neither flesh nor blood can inherit your kingdom. Your love alone brings us together, forever. Hear our prayers for the suffering: _____. **R**

The love of God has won. The new life has begun. **Amen.**

Texts: Genesis 3:8-15 or 1 Samuel 8:4-11 [12-15] 16-20 [11:14-15]   Psalm 130 or Psalm 138   2 Corinthians 4:13—5:1 Mark 3:20-35

Dates: June 5 – June 11

YEAR B

Time after Pentecost, Lectionary 11B

Responsive Sentence for the Sundays after Pentecost:
   Loving God, you hear our prayers: **You live among us.**

Lord God, you insert yourself into the affairs of humankind through Jesus, the Messiah, because no earthly leaders are able to redeem the world you love so deeply. You have spoken. You will accomplish it. **R**

Heavenly Father, even as you planted the majestic cedar tree and made it tall, so you also have brought us forth to bear fruit, in every age—even in old age. **R**

Lord Jesus Christ, help us look at you and others with the spiritual eyes of faith, knowing that we are your new creation. Even as you died and rose for us, urge us to live and care for others. **R**

You kingdom, Lord God, is a seed-planting kingdom. Help the kernel of life in every shell of every single body gathered here for worship, split and sprout like seed in good soil, always looking forward to your day of harvest. **R**

Holy Spirit, nations and leaders rise and fall like trees in a forest. In this age give us the wisdom to depend upon God's holy promises and commands, as our primary guides in life. **R**

Help us minister to those who need their health restored, their hope invigorated, their love rekindled. Bring us a joy greater than happiness, a love beyond imagination, and may our last illness bring us to your throne of grace. Hear us as we pray for one another: _____. **R**

The love of God has won. The new life has begun. **Amen.**

Texts: Ezekiel 17:22-24 or 1 Samuel 15:34—16:13   Psalm 92:1-4, 12-15 or Psalm 20   2 Corinthians 5:6-10 [11-13] 14-17   Mark 4:26-34

Dates: June 12 – June 18

Time after Pentecost, Lectionary 12B

Responsive Sentence for the Sundays after Pentecost:
Loving God, you hear our prayers: **You live among us.**

Heavenly Father, when you answered suffering Job out of the whirlwind, you challenged him to see you as Creator God. When we suffer and complain, help us note your wondrous work throughout the universe, and give you thanks for caring about us in the middle of it all. **R**

Lord of all nations, give us courage to trust you (like David before Goliath), to face danger unafraid, and to believe in your providence. **R**

Holy Spirit, mighty God, you still the storm with a whisper, for you are good. Still the storms that rage within us. **R**

Lord Jesus Christ, giver of God's grace, open our hearts to receive you in faith, to do your work on earth, and to give thanks for every daily opportunity to be your person. **R**

Lord Jesus Christ, as you calmed the sea, still the storms within us and around us, both in our personal lives and in our church lives. When you say, "Peace! Be still!," may we obey. **R**

Lord Jesus Christ, all of us know the pains of illness, separation, loneliness and death. Hear us as we name those with difficulties who need your Holy Spirit's presence, and your healing touch: _____. **R**

The love of God has won. The new life has begun. **Amen.**

Texts: Job 38:1-11 or 1 Samuel 17:[1a, 4-11, 19-23] 32-49 or 1 Samuel 17:57—18:5, 10-16   Psalm 107:1-3, 23-32 or Psalm 9:9-20 or Psalm 133   2 Corinthians 6:1-13   Mark 4:35-41

Dates: June 19 – June 25

YEAR B

Time after Pentecost, Lectionary 13B

Responsive Sentence for the Sundays after Pentecost:
   Loving God, you hear our prayers: **You live among us.**

Heavenly Father, when our yoke is heavy, when our patience is short, when silence is deafening, by your Holy Spirit remind us of your great faithfulness, and have compassion on us. **R**

Holy Spirit, you make the bonds of love between warriors on the field of battle "stronger than lions." Make our love for each other equally wonderful, as we struggle together on earth against all the forces of sin, death and the devil. **R**

Holy Spirit, hear our prayers when we are in the depths of despair, and reform our laments into praise, as we sense that the Lord Jesus Christ is bearing our burden. **R**

Lord Jesus Christ, as we share our gifts for your work, we do it because we first learned it from you. Receive our thanks for your Holy Spirit's encouragement to be generous, and bless all whose needs are attended to. **R**

Lord Jesus Christ, you know the cost of healing. You felt the power leave from yourself for the sake of others. Make us willing also to expend ourselves for another. **R**

Holy Spirit, you remind us that the seasons of our lives pass quickly, and at the end of our time, you have promised us a new home. Yet we are bold to ask for your mercies for those who need you here and now: _____. **R**

The love of God has won. The new life has begun. **Amen.**

Texts: 2 Samuel 1:1, 17-27 or Wisdom of Solomon 1:13-15; 2:23-24 or Lamentations 3:22-33   Psalm 130 or Psalm 30   2 Corinthians 8:7-15   Mark 5:21-43

Dates: June 26 – July 2

Time after Pentecost, Lectionary 14B

Responsive Sentence for the Sundays after Pentecost:
    Loving God, you hear our prayers: **You live among us.**

Heavenly Father, you knew that your prophets would often be ignored, yet you sent them out as messengers to speak your word with power. Open our ears, that we may hear your call to repentance. **R**

Lord God Almighty, King David became greater and greater, because you were with him. When he erred and forgot your presence, his greatness dimmed. We pray for obedience to you, ever-present God, so that we may live by faith, hope and love. **R**

Father, Son and Holy Spirit, you are great forever, and you guide us all our days. **R**

In our weaknesses, Lord Jesus Christ, we know you best. In our needs you find a way to be our Lord. **R**

Resistance to you, Lord Jesus Christ, never ends. You are often rejected, even as Our Father and the Holy Spirit are often rejected. Yet, you still love, heal, and visit your people. Help us see you in this place, at this very moment. **R**

As we name aloud those who need your healing, hear us as we also whisper our own name: _____. **R**

The love of God has won. The new life has begun. **Amen.**

Texts: Ezekiel 2:1-52 or Samuel 5:1-5, 9-10   Psalm 123 or Psalm 48   2 Corinthians 12:2-10   Mark 6:1-13

Dates: July 3 – July 9

YEAR B

Time after Pentecost, Lectionary 15B

Responsive Sentence for the Sundays after Pentecost:
    Loving God, you hear our prayers: **You live among us.**

Heavenly Father, you call ordinary people, like Amos, to witness. Help us to discern the message of those called by the church to speak, and to be open to hear your direct, personal call to serve. **R**

Holy Spirit, help us sense the Psalmist's joy in our lives. Let joy and faithfulness meet together. Let righteousness and peace kiss each other. **R**

Lord Jesus Christ, we know that our highest calling is to be children of God. Help us live as your adopted sons and daughters, as inheritors of your grace. **R**

Holy Spirit, although King Herod liked to hear John the Baptist preach, he was neither convinced nor converted by John's message. Guard us from careless listening to the Word of Life. **R**

Lord God, the desperate poor in this world, the deserted, the homeless and the hopeless are ever present. As we seek to meet basic needs for all, help us recognize that the face of our brother or sister in need is your holy face. **R**

Lord Jesus Christ, the poor in health need our prayers and our presence. Hear us name those we know who need your intervention: _____. **R**

The love of God has won. The new life has begun. **Amen.**

Texts: Amos 7:7-15 or 2 Samuel 6:1-5, 12b-19   Psalm 85:8-13 or Psalm 24   Ephesians 1:3-14   Mark 6:14-29

Dates: July 10 – July 16

Time after Pentecost, Lectionary 16B

Responsive Sentence for the Sundays after Pentecost:
Loving God, you hear our prayers: **You live among us.**

Lord God, raise up faithful pastors, priests, deacons and church leaders who love you more than all. Give to each of us the skill to be a shepherd in some small way, the will to be shepherded by other leaders, and the ability to trust the Good Shepherd over all. **R**

Father of our Lord Jesus Christ, you sent your Son to be the Messiah, and to build your church. As members of His kingdom, fill us with joy for His resurrected presence, His loving rule, and His kingdom yet to come. **R**

Holy Spirit, give us confidence when we walk through the valley of the shadow of death. Guard us from evil. Shepherd us with your rod and staff. Shower goodness and mercy upon us all the days of our lives. **R**

Lord Jesus Christ, you are our peace, granting access to God the Father through the Holy Spirit, making us citizens with the saints in the household of God. **R**

Lord Jesus, the apostles gathered around you and reported all that they had done and taught in your name. Help us see the good we do in your name and rejoice in being a helpmate of yours. **R**

Lord Jesus Christ, you invite us not only to work with you, but to rest with you. Though the desires of this world tire us, touch us, that we may be healed. Hear our prayers for those in need of your healing: _____. **R**

The love of God has won. The new life has begun. **Amen.**

Texts: Jeremiah 23:1-6 or 2 Samuel 7:1-14a   Psalm 23 or Psalm 89:20-37   Ephesians 2:11-22   Mark 6:30-34, 53-56

Dates: July 17 – July 23

Time after Pentecost, Lectionary 17B

Responsive Sentence for the Sundays after Pentecost:
  Loving God, you hear our prayers: **You live among us.**

Heavenly Father, caller of the prophets Elijah and Elisha, both workers of miracles, give us ears to hear your messengers who trust in you, knowing you will satisfy our every need. **R**

Like King David, Lord God, the sins of our passion often live after us with endless consequences. Yet, you still use us, love us, forgive us and let us be your people. **R**

Loving God, as you open wide your hands to satisfy our every need, open our hearts in gratitude toward you, and love toward one another. **R**

Holy Spirit, give us the wisdom of the Psalmist who knows to look for you, for every goodness, every deliverance, every tomorrow. **R**

Lord Jesus Christ, your love surpasses human knowledge, for it is higher, holier, wiser, and more beautiful than human words can describe. **R**

Lord Jesus, ever present in our next meal, and in our next rescue, open our eyes to see you always present with us. Hear, now, our prayers for others: _____. **R**

The love of God has won. The new life has begun. **Amen.**

Texts: 2 Kings 4:42-44 or 2 Samuel 11:1-15 Psalm 145:10-18 or Psalm 14 Ephesians 3:14-21 John 6:1-21

Dates: July 24 – July 30

Time after Pentecost, Lectionary 18B

Responsive Sentence for the Sundays after Pentecost:
    Loving God, you hear our prayers: **You live among us.**

Heavenly Father, when we complain that we cannot see your hand at work in our lives, remind us of the wilderness journey of the Israelites. Help us believe and live in patience, as your bigger and better plan is accomplished. **R**

Lord Jesus Christ, forgiver of our every sin, when we suffer the consequences of our own wrongdoing, give us courage to humbly confess like King David, "I have sinned against the Lord." **R**

Holy Spirit, when we eat our fill of food for yet another day, help us give you thanks by sharing our bounty with the less fortunate. **R**

Build us up in Love, Lord God, and help us use the gifts you've given to us, for your kingdom's sake. **R**

Lord Jesus Christ, true bread from heaven, send your Holy Spirit into our hearts that we may desire the food that endures for eternal life. **R**

Great Physician, turn our minds and hearts toward the physical and spiritual needs of all among us in pain and suffering: _____. **R**

The love of God has won. The new life has begun. **Amen.**

Texts: Exodus 16:2-4, 9-15 or 2 Samuel 11:26—12:13a   Psalm 78:23-29 or Psalm 51:1-12   Ephesians 4:1-16   John 6:24-35

Dates: July 31 – August 6

YEAR B

Time after Pentecost, Lectionary 19B

Responsive Sentence for the Sundays after Pentecost:
Loving God, you hear our prayers: **You live among us.**

Heavenly Father, when fatigue makes us ready to give up and die, speak to us, like an angel spoke to Elijah, and command us to "Get up, eat, and go on in the faith." **R**

Lord God Almighty, you give us people whom we come to love more than our own lives. Help us treasure one another, and remember that our beloved ones are gifts from you. **R**

Holy Spirit, as we obey the Psalmist's command: "Taste and see that the Lord is good," help us also take refuge in your presence and mercy. **R**

Lord Jesus Christ, help us model our lives after you, that we may refuse bitterness and anger, and replace them with kindness and love. **R**

Lord Jesus Christ, Bread of Life, even as you come to us in the Sacrament of Holy Communion, come to every moment of our every day, never leaving us hungry or alone. **R**

Lord Jesus, we bring real people with real needs to you in prayer, knowing that you are already caring for each of them. We name them, because we love them too: _____. **R**

The love of God has won. The new life has begun. **Amen.**

Texts: 1 Kings 19:4-8 or 2 Samuel 18:5-9, 15, 31-33   Psalm 34:1-8 or Psalm 130   Ephesians 4:25—5:2   John 6:35, 41-51

Dates: August 7 – August 13

Time after Pentecost, Lectionary 20B

Responsive Sentence for the Sundays after Pentecost:
    Loving God, you hear our prayers: **You live among us.**

Holy Spirit, fill us all with the wisdom of God, by walking in His ways and keeping His commandments all the days of our lives. **R**

Holy Spirit, fill us with true reverence for the Lord, that we may turn from evil, do good and seek peace. **R**

Holy Spirit, as we sing praises to God with our voices, help us sing with our hearts full of love. **R**

Lord Jesus Christ, living bread from heaven, as you were sent to us from the living Father, you have fed us with your own flesh and blood. As you live in us, so that we may live forever, help us live lives that reflect your love and grace. **R**

Help us, Heavenly Father, to see the whole world as your world, worthy of loving. Bring the nations together, that peace and good will may replace fear and rancor. **R**

Our frail bodies, Lord Jesus, need so much attention and healing. As we pray for one another, remind us of the new body promised each of us on the day of resurrection: _____. **R**

The love of God has won. The new life has begun. **Amen.**

Texts: Proverbs 9:1-6 or 1 Kings 2:10-12; 3:3-14   Psalm 34:9-14 or Psalm 111   Ephesians 5:15-20   John 6:51-58

Dates: August 14 – August 20

YEAR B

Time after Pentecost, Lectionary 21B

Responsive Sentence for the Sundays after Pentecost:
   Loving God, you hear our prayers: **You live among us.**

Lord God Almighty, may we revere and serve you, forsaking all other would-be gods. **R**

Holy Trinity, one God, you are so powerful that the highest heaven cannot contain you. Neither can our churches, our hearts nor our world hold you fast. Nevertheless, hear our prayers and pleas this day, for your love is far greater than our needs. **R**

Holy Spirit, comfort the brokenhearted among us with your promise of redemption and resurrection, for we believe we shall live forever in the house of the Lord. **R**

Arm us with your might, Lord God, else we will be defeated by evil. May your truth, peace, faith and holy Word guard us, inspire us and embolden us to be your people. **R**

Lord Jesus Christ, help us take no offense from your difficult teachings. You are the Holy One of God, and the Heavenly Father bids us come to you in faith. **R**

Lord God Almighty, this world delights in producing weapons of war. Forgive us our fear of one another, teach us to trust your Son, and bring peace to the hearts of all people. **R**

Among us are many counting on your goodness and mercy for hope and healing. Hear us as we name them: _____. **R**

The love of God has won. The new life has begun. **Amen.**

Texts: Joshua 24:1-2a, 14-18 or 1 Kings 8:[1, 6, 10-11] 22-30, 41-43   Psalm 34:15-22 or Psalm 84   Ephesians 6:10-20   John 6:56-69

Dates: August 21 – August 27

YEAR B

Time after Pentecost, Lectionary 22B

Responsive Sentence for the Sundays after Pentecost:
  Loving God, you hear our prayers: **You live among us.**

Heavenly Father, we thank you for your commandments. They guide us, they show us your will, and they help us live together in peace and respect for one another. **R**

Holy Spirit, open our ears to hear the voice of God's beloved Son, that we may live the love of Christ. **R**

Stir our hearts, Lord God, with noble songs of love, valor, and faithfulness, that our spirits may soar with the power of your mighty Word. **R**

As we listen to your admonitions, Holy Spirit, give us strength to act, to give, and to assist in the care of all in need, for we are your children, and we are all sisters and brothers, one to another. **R**

Lord Jesus Christ, more than our songs, our prayers, and our words, you desire our hearts. Become the love of our lives. **R**

Hear our prayers for our sisters and brothers in need: _____. **R**

The love of God has won. The new life has begun. **Amen.**

Texts: Deuteronomy 4:1-2, 6-9 or Song of Solomon 2:8-13   Psalm 15 or Psalm 45:1-2, 6-9   James 1:17-27   Mark 7:1-8, 14-15, 21-23

Dates: August 28 – September 3

Time after Pentecost, Lectionary 23B

Responsive Sentence for the Sundays after Pentecost:
Loving God, you hear our prayers: **You live among us.**

Heavenly Father, when we exile ourselves from you, rescue us. Open our deaf ears and our blind eyes. Quench our thirsty souls and repair our crippled feet, that we may rejoice in your coming. **R**

Whether we be rich or poor, Lord God, you especially plead the cause of the poor. Help us hear and heed that call with generosity and honor for all persons. **R**

Holy Spirit, lift our spirits to happiness when we sing the praise of the Lord, for He is with us and delights in our song. **R**

Holy Spirit, you invite us to have a living faith by caring for those in need. Keep us from begrudging help, for whether we be rich or poor we have great need for each other. **R**

Lord Jesus Christ, as you made the mute speak and the deaf hear; as you healed those with an unclean spirit, so touch us all where we suffer from spiritual deficit or physical pain. Hear us as we pray for one another: _____. **R**

The love of God has won. The new life has begun. **Amen.**

Texts: Isaiah 35:4-7a or Proverbs 22:1-2, 8-9, 22-23   Psalm 146 or Psalm 125   James 2:1-10 [11-13] 14-17   Mark 7:24-37

Dates: September 4 – September 10

Time after Pentecost, Lectionary 24B

Responsive Sentence for the Sundays after Pentecost:
  Loving God, you hear our prayers: **You live among us.**

Heavenly Father, by your Word you created the universe, and through your prophet Isaiah you gave the gift of sustaining the weary with a word. Open our ears and our weary hearts to receive your spoken Word. **R**

Holy Spirit, your Wisdom is life. Make us eager recipients of your Word, that we may live life wisely. **R**

You hear our voices, Lord God. You listen to our prayers. Give us wisdom to call upon you when sorrow, death or adversity nears, that we may receive your grace. **R**

Heavenly Father, your judgments are true and righteous. As the Psalmist reports, your teachings, commandments and judgments are clear, "and are more to be desired than gold." Give us the will to treasure them. **R**

Lord Jesus Christ, you clearly suffered as the Messiah. As we help others bear their crosses in life, make us receptive to receive ministry from whomever will help us carry our own burdens. **R**

Make us mindful, Holy Spirit, of the deep sufferings of the poor, the lonely and the afraid in every church, town, city and country. Give us joy in serving others. **R**

We bring before you specific people with special needs that require divine care. Hear us as we name them: _____. **R**

The love of God has won. The new life has begun. **Amen.**

Texts: Isaiah 50:4-9a or Proverbs 1:20-33   Psalm 116:1-9 or Psalm 19 or Wisdom of Solomon 7:26—8:1   James 3:1-12   Mark 8:27-38

Dates: September 11 – September 17

YEAR B

Time after Pentecost, Lectionary 25B

Responsive Sentence for the Sundays after Pentecost:
Loving God, you hear our prayers: **You live among us.**

Heavenly Father, as we commit our collective and personal ministries into your care, protect us from those who would fault us or use us, for we seek to be your faithful disciples. **R**

Holy Spirit, fill us with courage when we find ourselves or our church dismissed as irrelevant by those who despise the preaching of the gospel and the teaching of the Word. **R**

Keep us from envy and selfish ambition, Lord God. Help us be peacemakers in this world of disorder and conflict. As we submit ourselves to you, draw near to us. **R**

Lord Jesus Christ, help us from seeking fame and superiority over others. Instead, make us your willing servants. **R**

We pray for the church catholic, Holy Spirit, as you gather us to grow in the faith, give thanks for your presence, and give our gifts for service in this world. **R**

Though disease plagues us, your healing saves us from despair. Hear us as we name those among us in need: _____. **R**

The love of God has won. The new life has begun. **Amen.**

Texts: Jeremiah 11:18-20 or Wisdom of Solomon 1:16—2:1, 12-22 or Proverbs 31:10-31   Psalm 54 or Psalm 1   James 3:13—4:3, 7-8a   Mark 9:30-37

Dates: September 18 – September 24

Time after Pentecost, Lectionary 26B

Responsive Sentence for the Sundays after Pentecost:
Loving God, you hear our prayers: **You live among us.**

Heavenly Father, help us when our needs are confused with our desires and cravings, like those who wanted more than simply manna in the wilderness. Give us joy in receiving from your hand what is most necessary. **R**

Lord God, even as Esther thwarted the evil plans of those planning wickedness, continue to foil the plots and schemes of those who would harm others. **R**

Revive our souls, Holy Spirit, as we listen to the Word, that the words of our mouths and the meditations of our hearts are acceptable to you. **R**

Lord Jesus Christ, help us be your church at work as we pray, sing songs of praise, confess our sins, and return to you in joy. **R**

Lord Jesus Christ, we wish to be your disciples in ways acceptable to you. Guide us as we plan to be your church in this place, now, and in the days to come. **R**

Lord Jesus Christ, you tell us to be the salt of the earth. Hear us as we seek to preserve life, add zest, and be healing agents as we pray for others by name: _____. **R**

The love of God has won. The new life has begun. **Amen.**

Texts: Numbers 11:4-6, 10-16, 24-29 or Esther 7:1-6, 9-10; 9:20-22   Psalm 19:7-14 or Psalm 124   James 5:13-20   Mark 9:38-50

Dates: September 25 – October 1

Time after Pentecost, Lectionary 27B

Responsive Sentence for the Sundays after Pentecost:
    Loving God, you hear our prayers: **You live among us.**

Heavenly Father, Creator of all that is seen and unseen, we rejoice as your men and women, created in your image, and after your likeness, becoming one flesh together. **R**

Lord Jesus Christ, you were tested like Job, but endured through your suffering even unto death on the cross. Help us understand the cost of our atonement, and to thank you for it by lives devoted to your resurrected presence among us. **R**

O Lord, our God, when we consider all that you have made, we stand in awe that you are not only mindful of us, but also consider us worthy of your honor and glory. How majestic is your name in all the earth. **R**

Lord Jesus Christ, in your act of sanctification, you were brought very low in order to taste suffering and death for us. We rejoice to know that your Father is Our Father. Out of love you are not ashamed to call us your brothers and sisters. **R**

Lord Jesus, even as you lifted a child up and taught that children, women and men are equal, help us enter your kingdom like a child, trusting you with every single step of the way. **R**

Lord Jesus, hear us name the names of those who need deliverance and healing: _____. **R**

The love of God has won. The new life has begun. **Amen.**

Texts: Genesis 2:18-24 or Job 1:1; 2:1-10   Psalm 8 or Psalm 26   Hebrews 1:1-4; 2:5-12   Mark 10:2-16

Dates: October 2 – October 8

Time after Pentecost, Lectionary 28B

Responsive Sentence for the Sundays after Pentecost:
   Loving God, you hear our prayers: **You live among us.**

Lord God, you are the God of justice, caring for the poor, the wronged, the used and the ignored. Open our eyes to see every human in need as your child, our sister, or our brother. Inspire us to care the most for those who have the least. **R**

Holy Spirit, help us see ourselves in the bitter lament of Job, who knows you are listening but cannot sense your nearness nor the reason for his suffering. Deliver us, like you delivered him. **R**

Holy Spirit, we know our days are numbered. Help us live in holy expectation of your coming. **R**

Heavenly Father, when we feel forsaken, lift up our eyes to see life continuing, your new world dawning, and an everlasting reunion assured. **R**

Lord Jesus Christ, tested like we are but without sin, give us boldness to approach your throne of grace, hand extended, love expected. **R**

Lord Jesus, we worry with the disciples that our wealth is in the way. Knowing how hard it is for the rich to enter the kingdom of God, console us with the truth that everything is possible by God's grace. **R**

Hear us as we pray for those who need help and healing: _____. **R**

The love of God has won. The new life has begun. **Amen.**

Texts: Amos 5:6-7, 10-15 or Job 23:1-9, 16-17   Psalm 90:12-17 or Psalm 22:1-15   Hebrews 4:12-16   Mark 10:17-31

Dates: October 9 – October 15

Time after Pentecost, Lectionary 29B

Responsive Sentence for the Sundays after Pentecost:
　　Loving God, you hear our prayers:　　**You live among us.**

Lord Jesus Christ, Our Redeemer, foretold by Isaiah as the bearer of our sins, forgive us when we stray, and bring us back to the fold. **R**

Heavenly Father, you gave Job the private audience he wanted to have with you. Be gentle with us when we foolishly ask for more than we can handle. **R**

Holy Spirit, when angels attend to us, make us aware that such love is your tender care. **R**

Lord Jesus Christ, High Priest, ever obedient to God the Father, to whom you prayed with loud cries and tears, hear our anguish in times of distress, and walk with us through every fear. **R**

Lord Jesus, when we seek personal glory instead of sacrificial service, forgive us our desire for glory, all of which belongs to you, and to you alone. **R**

Holy Spirit, look with kindness at this family of faith gathered here for worship, and help us be God's hands in the world outside this sanctuary. **R**

For those among us who are sick, hear our ardent prayers for your will to be done: _____. **R**

The love of God has won. The new life has begun. **Amen.**

Texts:　Isaiah 53:4-12 or Job 38:1-7 [34-41]　Psalm 91:9-16 or Psalm 104:1-9, 24　Hebrews 5:1-10
Mark 10:35-45

Dates:　October 16 – October 22

Time after Pentecost, Lectionary 30B

Responsive Sentence for the Sundays after Pentecost:
   Loving God, you hear our prayers: **You live among us.**

Heavenly Father, like Job, when we ask for your presence and intervention, we may end up on our knees, astounded at your greatness, and humbled by our own unworthiness. **R**

Holy Spirit, when we tearfully share our hopes and dreams with you, you promise a harvest of joy. Fill us with expectations of your goodness. **R**

Lord Jesus Christ, high priest and intercessor for our sins, help us live as your children, trusting that we are also children of the Heavenly Father. **R**

Lord Jesus, healer of Bartimaeus' blindness, help us see you in this world active in love, and help us see you by our side, so we may walk your way without stumbling. **R**

Lord Jesus, Great Physician, hear now the names of those we know who need your healing: _____. **R**

The love of God has won. The new life has begun. **Amen.**

Texts: Job 42:1-6, 10-17 or Jeremiah 31:7-9   Psalm 34:1-8 [19-22] or Psalm 126   Hebrews 7:23-28   Mark 10:46-52

Dates: October 23 – October 29

Reformation Sunday

Responsive Sentence for Reformation Sunday:
   We hear God's holy invitation: **"Be still and know that I am God."**

Heavenly Father, forgiver of our every sin, in Christ we are your new people. Your law is written on our minds and hearts. Your gospel is in the marrow of our bones. Our souls exalt with the good news of your new covenant with us. **R**

Lord God, our refuge and strength, your wondrous works make wars cease, plots fail, evil kingdoms totter. **R**

Lord Jesus Christ, through your work of atonement for us, the righteousness of God has been disclosed apart from the law. We dare not boast except in your loving and sacrificial death for our salvation. **R**

Holy Spirit, inspire us with the truth that makes us free from fear, free from eternal death, free to be your disciples of grace, love, joy, peace and patience. **R**

In the noise of our clamoring cities and factories, in the loud debates of opinion and politics, reform us by quieting all fears and doubts as we listen for you. **R**

Christ our King, weeping over Jerusalem, praying for us to Our Father, promising a crucified thief paradise, providing family beneath the cross for Mary your mother, and for John your disciple, we pray that you will care for us too. **R**

Hear our gratitude for hospitals, laboratories, institutions of learning; for nurses and doctors and family members who attend to our needs, and for churches like this gathering, where we boldly name the names of those who need your healing touch: _____. **R**

Reform us, make us your saints in this church militant, and in the life to come, make us your saints in the church triumphant. Be our one and only King.
Amen.

Texts: Jeremiah 31:31-34   Psalm 46   Romans 3:19-28   John 8:31-36

All Saints Sunday

Responsive Sentence for All Saints Sunday:
We hear God's holy invitation: **"Be still and know that I am God."**

Almighty God, the souls of all your saints are in your hands. Give us the eyes of the wise who pity the foolish, who think that death is forever. As you test us in the furnace of hard experience, help us shine forth as your sparks of light and love in a dark and needy world. **R**

Lord God, most tender and Holy Spirit, as you wipe away our tears of mourning help us see the feast that is coming, at your table and in your heaven. Strong and mighty Lord, give us voice to rejoice and be glad in the salvation of our souls. **R**

Lord of hosts, King of Glory, this earth is your earth, and all who live upon it are yours. Open our eyes to see the heavenly gates lift up, and the doors swing wide open as you come into our lives, strong and mighty. **R**

Lord Jesus Christ, Our Savior, you came and lived among us to fulfill the Scripture that the home of God is among mortals. Help us see the day when tears of joy replace those of sadness, for the new Jerusalem descends from above, and death will be no more. **R**

Holy Spirit, give us the heart to see Jesus weeping over our sorrows. Unbind us and let us live anew, like Lazarus from the tomb, believing that you have been sent by Our Father and Your Father. **R**

For all the saints, living on earth or in the hereafter, we rejoice in your power to heal, inspire and resurrect. Hear us as we name those whom you have placed in our lives to love, both in this world and the next: _____. **R**

Reform us, make us your saints in this church militant, and in the life to come, make us your saints in the church triumphant. Be our one and only King. **Amen.**

Texts: Wisdom of Solomon 3:1-9 or Isaiah 25:6-9   Psalm 24   Revelation 21:1-6a   John 11:32-44

YEAR B

Time after Pentecost, Lectionary 31B

Responsive Sentence for the Sundays after Pentecost:
   Loving God, you hear our prayers: **You live among us.**

Heavenly Father, bind us with your love as we seek with heart, mind and might to know you as our only Lord and God. **R**

Holy Spirit, as Ruth and Naomi bonded in love, wherever you go, take us with you, and do not let death separate us, one from the other. **R**

Lord Jesus Christ, high priest, you offered yourself as the sacrifice for our sin, and we ask you to purify our hearts and minds, that we may joyfully worship the living God. **R**

Lord Jesus, you take our endless questions and replace them with the mandate to love God and to love one another. Remind us how close we are to the kingdom of God when, by grace, we are able to love like you love. **R**

God of every land, every planet, every galaxy, and every living soul, we cannot escape your presence, and we ask you to make us glad that this is so. **R**

Generations rise and fall before you, Lord God, like sunrise and sunset. You alone know what time it is in our lifespan. We bring the names of people of all ages who need your help, and we ask that we may see your will working by what is done for each of them: _____. **R**

The love of God has won. The new life has begun. **Amen.**

Texts: Ruth 1:1-18 or Deuteronomy 6:1-9   Psalm 146 or Psalm 119:1-8   Hebrews 9:11-14   Mark 12:28-34

Dates: October 30 – November 5

Time after Pentecost, Lectionary 32B

Responsive Sentence for the Sundays after Pentecost:
   Loving God, you hear our prayers: **You live among us.**

Lord God Almighty, as you intervene in the affairs of nations, because you care what nations do, guard and protect us from one another. **R**

Heavenly Father, simple love between Ruth and Naomi is used by you for greater purposes. No one but you could know that Ruth would be King David's grandmother! Help us believe in your providence. **R**

Holy Spirit, one God, as we rely on you alone for justice, mercy and truth in this world, hear our praise for your goodness. **R**

Lord Jesus Christ, high priest, in the very presence of God in heaven on our behalf, we eagerly wait for your return with salvation in hand. **R**

Lord Jesus Christ, like the widow in the temple who gave all she had, inspire us to give without worry about the worthiness of churches, states, institutions or individuals. Receive our gifts as love offerings. **R**

Have mercy on all whom we name in prayer, O Lord. You alone know what is best for each: _____. **R**

The love of God has won. The new life has begun. **Amen.**

Texts: Ruth 3:1-5; 4:13-17 or 1 Kings 17:8-16   Psalm 127 or Psalm 146   Hebrews 9:24-28   Mark 12:38-44

Dates: November 6 – November 12

YEAR B

Time after Pentecost, Lectionary 33B

Responsive Sentence for the Sundays after Pentecost:
    Loving God, you hear our prayers: **You live among us.**

Father God, at the end of time as we know it, you will be there. Help us, through the power of the Holy Spirit, to have no fear of that day or of that hour, for your Son, Jesus, our Savior, will be there for us. **R**

Lord God Almighty, even as you listened to Hannah as she poured out her soul to you in despair, hear our prayers, and use us as you used her in your holy work. **R**

Holy Spirit, keep us from making gods out of our needs and desires, and teach us to take refuge in your strength and counsel. **R**

Lord Jesus Christ, high priest, by your Holy Spirit you remember our sins no more. May we worship with a clean heart full of faith, and seek to do good works for and with one another, for the day of your return approaches. **R**

Lord Jesus Christ, you call all that we fear about the end of time mere "birth pangs." Help us dread the end as little as we worried about our first birth. You will be present. **R**

Come, Lord Jesus, into the lives of those who need healing: _____. **R**

The love of God has won. The new life has begun. **Amen.**

Texts: 1 Samuel 1:4-20 or Daniel 12:1-3   1 Samuel 2:1-10 or Psalm 16   Hebrews 10:11-14 [15-18] 19-25 Mark 13:1-8

Dates: November 13 – November 19

Christ the King, Lectionary 34B

Responsive Sentence for Christ the King:
    Rejoice to know: **Christ is King**

Christ our King, Messiah and Judge, you fulfill Daniel's prophesy and your Kingship shall never end. When you return, remember us. **R**

Mighty Lord, King forever, even as you fulfill the kingship of David as God's Messiah, be King of our lives. **R**

Lord Jesus Christ, ruler of the kings of the earth, you are the firstborn from the dead. Fill us with the joyful expectation of your return in glory. **R**

Lord Jesus Christ, your second coming is not going to be missed. Every eye will see you, even those who crucified you. Come now, into our lives, that your coming as King will be all joy for us. **R**

Jesus, born to be King of a realm greater than earth, give us the raw courage to listen to your voice and to obey your commands. **R**

We confess, Holy Spirit, that we sometimes balk at the notion of "kingship," wishing things might be accomplished in a more "cooperative" mode. Forgive us for thinking we don't need your divine Kingly rule. **R**

Christ our King, you invite us to approach your throne and ask for healing. Hear us as we name those who need your healing touch: _____. **R**

Reform us, make us your saints in this church militant, and in the life to come, make us your saints in the church triumphant. Be our one and only King. **Amen.**

Texts: 2 Samuel 23:1-7 or Daniel 7:9-10, 13-14   Psalm 132:1-12 [13-18] or Psalm 93   Revelation 1:4b-8 John 18:33-37

Dates: November 20 – November 26

YEAR B

1st Sunday of Advent

Responsive Sentence for Advent:
    Stir up your power and come: **Be born anew in us.**

Righteous God, you fulfill your promises with the coming of the righteous Branch, Jesus Christ. As we follow His teachings, help us accept new ways of being just and righteous. **R**

Remember us, Lord God, not by our transgressions, but according to your steadfast love. **R**

Holy Spirit, strengthen our hearts in holiness that we may joyfully look forward to the coming of Jesus with all His saints. **R**

Lord Jesus, when all around us is disaster and gloom, you tell us to look up, for then we shall see you coming in power and great glory. **R**

Holy Spirit, as we contemplate the ending of the world, prepare us to be alert, that we may be able to stand before the Son of Man, rejoicing in His love, strength and glory. **R**

Disease and death, remind us, Lord God, that we still have very real physical needs. Hear our prayers for those who need your healing: _____. **R**

We look with joy to the coming of Jesus. **Amen.**

Texts: Jeremiah 33:14-16   Psalm 25:1-10   1 Thessalonians 3:9-13   Luke 21:25-36

2nd Sunday of Advent

Responsive Sentence for Advent:
    Stir up your power and come: **Be born anew in us.**

Heavenly Father, we thank you for your prophets like Malachi who foretold the coming of your Son. When we feel the heat of the gospel forming our hearts to be more loving, may we give thanks for Jesus, the refiner and purifier of our souls. **R**

Holy Spirit, you let the Psalmist acknowledge the prophet of the Most High, Jesus, who prepares the Way. Guide our feet into the way of peace. **R**

Holy Spirit, as the people of the Christian church at Phillipi held St. Paul close to heart, fill us with love for all those who serve your holy church. **R**

Lord Jesus Christ, you heard John the Baptist preach about your coming. May all of us see the salvation of God through your gifts of baptism and forgiveness. **R**

As Christmas nears, Heavenly Father, remind us of our own birthdays into the faith. **R**

Lord Jesus Christ, ever present in the lives of both the strong and the weak, heal those suffering from any adversity: _____. **R**

We look with joy to the coming of Jesus. **Amen.**

Texts: Baruch 5:1-9 or Malachi 3:1-4   Luke 1:68-79   Philippians 1:3-11   Luke 3:1-6

3rd Sunday of Advent

Responsive Sentence for Advent:
    Stir up your power and come: **Be born anew in us.**

Heavenly Father, thank you for sending us prophets, priests and kings, but it is primarily your Son, the Lord Jesus Christ, whom we cannot resist. Help us follow Him as we are led to your heavenly arms. **R**

Great is your faithfulness, Lord God Almighty. Hear us as we sing for joy, pray with passion, and live the life of those who know the surety of the future. **R**

Even as St. Paul called us to be gentle, give us the wisdom to not worry about anything, for you are the God of Peace. **R**

Lord Jesus Christ, John the Baptist, earth's greatest preacher, knew he was unworthy to untie your sandals. In all our attempts to use words with power and bravado, remind us that you are the Great Word incarnate. **R**

You are coming soon, Lord Jesus, not only in the incarnation we know as Christmas, but especially by your birthing into our very own lives this day. **R**

We name those who love you, wonder about you, forget you, but need you: _____. **R**

We look with joy to the coming of Jesus. **Amen.**

Texts: Zephaniah 3:14-20   Isaiah 12:2-6   Philippians 4:4-7   Luke 3:7-18

YEAR C

4th Sunday of Advent

Responsive Sentence for Advent:
    Stir up your power and come: **Be born anew in us.**

Heavenly Father, sender of Jesus the Shepherd-King, help us, both as a flock and as one of your sheep, to follow the Prince of Peace to the ends of the earth. **R**

Holy Spirit, God among us, you feed the hungry, you lift high the lowly, and you keep your promises to be our God forever. Do not let our doubts or our sin make us go away empty from your presence. **R**

Lord Jesus Christ, holy priest, by your sacrifice we are made your people. Help us seek the changing of our wills, from our own selfish way to your most noble way of sacrifice and love. **R**

Holy Spirit, when you come to visit us, like you went to visit Mary, give us an open heart, a song of praise, and a willingness to be used in ways that are best for your kingdom. **R**

Lord Jesus Christ, may the love of your mother, Mary, inspire all of us who have been chosen to be parents, aunts, uncles, sisters, brothers, wives or husbands to see family as a most precious gift of love. **R**

Intrude into our grieving world, Great Physician, where disease is ever present and bring healing for those whom we name before you: _____. **R**

We look with joy to the coming of Jesus. **Amen.**

Texts: Micah 5:2-5a   Luke 1:46b-55 or Psalm 80:1-7   Hebrews 10:5-10   Luke 1:39-45 [46-55]

Nativity of Our Lord
Christmas Eve, December 24th

Responsive Sentence for Christmas
    Once born in Bethlehem: **Be born in us today.**

We proclaim with the Psalmist: "The Lord is king! The world is firmly established; it shall never be moved. He will judge the peoples with equity." **R**

Let the heavens be glad, and let the earth rejoice, for the Lord is coming tonight. **R**

Unto us a child is given, and He is named Wonderful Counselor, Mighty God, Everlasting Father, Prince of Peace. **R**

In these days help us hear the angel's message: "Do not be afraid, the news is good, for this is the day of Messiah's birth. **R**

Hear our songs this night as we join in the chorus of the Heavenly Hosts, praising God and singing, "Glory to God in the highest, and peace to God's people on earth!" **R**

Thank you Father God, for your Son. Thank you Holy Spirit, for calling us to belief. Thank you, Lord Jesus Christ, for coming to do your Godly work on earth for us. **R**

Let your light shine upon us and we shall be saved. **Amen.**

Texts: Isaiah 9:2-7   Psalm 96   Titus 2:11-14   Luke 2:1-14 [15-20]

YEAR C

Nativity of Our Lord
Christmas Day, December 25th

Responsive Sentence for Christmas
  Once born in Bethlehem: **Be born in us today.**

Heavenly Father, your prophet, Isaiah, counseled his people to give you no rest, to badger you with prayers, so that your ultimate will would come quickly. Hear us plead for your New Jerusalem, the very coming of Christ again. **R**

Holy God, guard the lives of your saints, protect us from disaster and wrongdoing. Let us sing and rejoice in this world, even while suffering continues. **R**

Holy Spirit, pour grace upon us in such a torrent that we will be reminded of our baptisms, cleansed by your swift forgiveness, and be swept into the company of the heirs of eternal life. **R**

Lord Jesus Christ, in the fulness of time, you came into this world. Come, now, into our lives, that we may rejoice in sharing the presence of God in this place and at this hour. **R**

Heavenly Father, it was poor shepherds in the field who heard the angels sing. By faith, give us a poor shepherd's eyes and ears, that we may proclaim your coming as well. **R**

We look, Lord Jesus, at mangers and stalls and marvel at the ways of the Father God. Come to us in the most impoverished part of our lives, that we may believe and rejoice. **R**

Lord Jesus, we name persons who are experiencing the uncertainty of illness, trusting you will meet them in their need: _____. **R**

Let your light shine upon us and we shall be saved. **Amen.**

Texts: Isaiah 62:6-12   Psalm 97   Titus 3:4-7   Luke 2:[1-7] 8-20

1st Sunday after Christmas Day

Responsive Sentence for Christmas
    Once born in Bethlehem: **Be born in us today.**

Heavenly Father, you accepted the ministries of the boy, Samuel. Give us confidence that our serving is received by you in joy, regardless of our age. **R**

Sun, moon, stars and angels; fire, hail, snow and fog; mountains, hills, fruit trees and cedars; wild beasts, birds, cattle and creeping things—all praise your name. Hear our voices join their song. **R**

Holy Spirit, you invite us to clothe ourselves with love. As we clothe ourselves according to your command, may compassion, kindness, humility, gentleness and patience be our gift to others. **R**

Lord Jesus, even as a child, Mary and Joseph took you to the church of their time so that you might know the family of faith beyond both of them. Help us bring our children to church, and into the awareness of the greater family of God. **R**

Lord Jesus, lover of the Heavenly Father's house, increase our wisdom that we may please you with our love. **R**

Even as Mary treasured in her heart the life of Jesus, so we treasure those whom we name before you, as gifts from you to care for: _____. **R**

Let your light shine upon us and we shall be saved. **Amen.**

Texts: 1 Samuel 2:18-20, 26   Psalm 148   Colossians 3:12-17   Luke 2:41-52

YEAR C

2nd Sunday after Christmas Day

Responsive Sentence for Christmas
    Once born in Bethlehem: **Be born in us today.**

Almighty God, you comfort us and turn our mourning into joy when you guide us back into your presence. Help us "be radiant with the goodness of the LORD." **R**

Holy Spirit, bless our children, grant us peace, give favorable weather and water to all, and help us love your most holy word. **R**

Heavenly Father, you chose us before the foundation of the world to be blessed in Christ with the spirituality of love. As you have adopted us, help us revel in your care, your gifts, your holy will, and your plan for our eternal inheritance. **R**

Lord Jesus Christ, so close to the Heavenly Father's heart, give us the gift to believe that you have made us "children of God." **R**

Be born anew in us, Lord Jesus, that your Holy Spirit may be as real to us as our own breath, our own beating heart, our own sense of the Divine. **R**

We remember to bring before you all the saints who suffer for the faith, and all in any sort of need. Hear us as we recall each of them by name: _____. **R**

Let your light shine upon us and we shall be saved. **Amen.**

Texts: Jeremiah 31:7-14 or Sirach 24:1-12   Psalm 147:12-20 or Wisdom of Solomon 10:15-21   Ephesians 1:3-14
John 1:[1-9] 10-18

The Epiphany of Our Lord
January 6th

Responsive Sentence for the Epiphany of Our Lord:
   Let us walk: **In the light of the Lord.**

Heavenly Father, you sent the Light of the World, Jesus Christ, to witness and to die in Jerusalem for the sins of the world. Give us eyes to see the Light that shall not be extinguished by the darkness of any night. **R**

Fill us, Holy Spirit, with justice and compassion for all, that we may we give you thanks for moving our hearts, minds and hands to care for one another. **R**

Lord Jesus Christ, make us prisoners of the gospel, that we might proclaim the boundless riches of your grace for all people. **R**

Lord Jesus, even as the magi from the East gave gifts of gold, frankincense and myrrh, receive our humble gifts, as we recognize you as King of kings, and Lord of lords. **R**

Holy Spirit, protect the church from harm, the faith from wrong, and all of us who seek to follow Jesus, just like you protected the wise men from the East. **R**

Lord Jesus, born beneath the Star of the East, healer of our every woe, hear us as we pray for one another: _____. **R**

Light of the world, shine brightly. **Amen.**

   Texts: Isaiah 60:1-6   Psalm 72:1-7, 10-14   Ephesians 3:1-12   Matthew 2:1-12

YEAR C

Baptism of Our Lord
1st Sunday after Epiphany

Responsive Sentence for the Sundays after Epiphany:
   Let us walk: **In the light of the Lord.**

Almighty God, you have created us as your saints, formed us as your church, and redeemed us from the enemy by the work of Jesus Christ. Remove all fear from our lives, for we belong to you. **R**

Voice of the Lord, powerful voice, like lightning and thunder, give strength to your people. **R**

Holy Spirit, we ask you to come into our lives in unmistakable ways, that we may recognize you and be your ambassador of love. **R**

Jesus, Beloved Son of God, send your Holy Spirit upon us that we may faithfully be your people. **R**

We remember that we are baptized, Lord Jesus, and adopted as daughters and sons of God Most High. In that assurance, hear our prayer of thanksgiving. **R**

As we pray for those in need, remind us that we have nothing to fear, for we belong to you: _____. **R**

Light of the world, shine brightly. **Amen.**

Texts: Isaiah 43:1-7   Psalm 29   Acts 8:14-17   Luke 3:15-17, 21-22

2nd Sunday after Epiphany

Responsive Sentence for the Sundays after Epiphany:
   Let us walk: **In the light of the Lord.**

Rejoice over us, Lord God, for we belong to you, and seek to be your faithful people. **R**

Priceless is your love, Lord God, and abundant are your gifts. As you continue your loving kindness toward us, give us the skill and the will to do the same for others. **R**

Lord Jesus Christ, help us look upon each other as gifted persons of your own choosing, so that none of us feel inferior or superior to another, but give simple thanks for the special gift you have given each of us. **R**

Lord Jesus, as you revealed your glory through miracles, reveal yourself through the miracle of faith at work in our lives. **R**

Heavenly Father, give us the faith to see you at work in every land, in every faith, and in every soul that looks toward you for love, inspiration, and direction. **R**

Remembering your power to heal, we bring before you those with need: _____. **R**

Light of the world, shine brightly. **Amen.**

Texts: Isaiah 62:1-5   Psalm 36:5-10   1 Corinthians 12:1-11   John 2:1-11

YEAR C

3rd Sunday after Epiphany

Responsive Sentence for the Sundays after Epiphany:
    Let us walk: **In the light of the Lord.**

Heavenly Father, when we are overwhelmed and mournful, remind us of your joy for us, and fill us with your strength. **R**

Holy Spirit, give us ears to hear the Lord through the beauty of the sky, the history of your presence in all times, and in the commandments given for our own good. **R**

Lord Jesus Christ, help us give thanks for every gift you've given to us, and may we use our special gifts for your glory. **R**

Lord Jesus, bringer of good news to all of us who are poor in faith, open our eyes, our ears and our hearts to receive your message of joy. **R**

When we struggle with the world's wayward directions, with politics held higher than truth, give us a spirit of discernment, Holy Spirit, that we may keep our focus on you. **R**

We bring before you all who are weary with bodies worn from age and disease. Be the healer, the comforter, and the hope for those whom we name before you: _____. **R**

Light of the world, shine brightly. **Amen.**

Texts: Nehemiah 8:1-3, 5-6, 8-10   Psalm 19   1 Corinthians 12:12-31a   Luke 4:14-21

4th Sunday after Epiphany

Responsive Sentence for the Sundays after Epiphany:
  Let us walk: **In the light of the Lord.**

Lord God Almighty, as with Jeremiah, you planned to use us before we were born. Give us a vision of your providence over time itself, that in our brief earthly lifespans, we may be your useful persons. **R**

Lord Jesus Christ, Hope Incarnate, sustain us with love, fill us with confidence, and hear the sound of our praise. **R**

Holy Spirit, as you nurture us in life and we pass from childhood to adulthood, fill us with an active faith, a dauntless hope and a love so real that we know it could only have come from you. **R**

Lord Jesus Christ, when we seek your favor like a famous hometown son or daughter, you know it's not you we love, but what you might do for us. As you teach us your humble ways, and decide how best to reach us, give us the Holy Spirit's eye to see you at work among us. **R**

Forbid us, Lord, from ever wanting to be rid of you, like an angry mob who would have thrown you over a cliff. As you turn away and pass among us, forgive all who know neither the cost nor the depth of your love. **R**

We ask you, out of love for one another, to visit those among us who need your help: _____. **R**

Light of the world, shine brightly. **Amen.**

Texts: Jeremiah 1:4-10   Psalm 71:1-6   1 Corinthians 13:1-13   Luke 4:21-30

5th Sunday after Epiphany

Responsive Sentence for the Sundays after Epiphany:
  Let us walk: **In the light of the Lord.**

Heavenly Father, sometimes we are reluctant to believe you are calling us, individually, or as a church, because we are aware of our sinfulness. Nevertheless, you remind us that all who serve you are imperfect persons of your graceful choosing. **R**

Great High God, as you care for the lowly, make good your purposes for us, and let your Holy Spirit remind us that you do not abandon the works of your hands. **R**

Lord Jesus Christ, when we work hard on your behalf to witness to the faith, remind us that it is the grace of God within us that is working the hardest. **R**

Lord Jesus Christ, as the disciples caught more fish than they could ever imagine, and then became fishers of people, cast your net upon us, reel us in, and let us proudly be known as "caught by Christ." **R**

Holy Spirit, never content to let the gathering of the people be all that is required of us, send us out from this place to be fishers of people. **R**

Lord Jesus, we thank you for the cures you make possible through wise physicians, surgery, and good medicine. Now, by the power of your healing Word, hear the names of those among us in need: _____. **R**

Light of the world, shine brightly. **Amen.**

Texts: Isaiah 6:1-8 [9-13]   Psalm 138   1 Corinthians 15:1-11   Luke 5:1-11

6th Sunday after Epiphany

Responsive Sentence for the Sundays after Epiphany:
    Let us walk: **In the light of the Lord.**

Lord God Almighty, help us be like a tree planted by the living water, by setting our roots deep into the life of the living Christ. **R**

Watch over us, Heavenly Father, and guide us on the path with Christ our Lord. **R**

Resurrected Lord, into your hands we have committed all whom we have loved on earth, and lost for a time. Now, make our faith alive, that we may live life joyfully, knowing that the Day of Resurrection is near. **R**

Lord Jesus, greatest teacher, greatest preacher, your beatitudes touch us with assurance, and challenge us to be brave. Help us look forward to the day when we shall rejoice and leap for joy. **R**

Holy Spirit, open our minds and hearts to the messages of Jesus, so that our inspiration might be followed by faithfully living by His promises to return, restore, and resurrect all of us. **R**

We remember those who think they may have lost faith, those who struggle with the physicality of this life, and those who are weary and ill. Hear us pray for one another: _____. **R**

Light of the world, shine upon us. **Amen.**

Texts: Jeremiah 17:5-10   Psalm 1   1 Corinthians 15:12-20   Luke 6:17-26

YEAR C

7th Sunday after Epiphany

Responsive Sentence for the Sundays after Epiphany:
  Let us walk: **In the light of the Lord.**

Heavenly Father, even as you made good out of what was intended for evil by Joseph's brothers, so give us a heart like Joseph to see you working in, through, and past the hard events of our own lives. **R**

Holy Spirit, keep us from fretting by trusting in the Lord, for He will act. **R**

Holy Spirit, help us understand that the kingdom of God is ours as an imperishable gift, simply because God loves us. **R**

Lord Jesus Christ, beyond flesh and blood in your resurrected body, we are in your hands, now and forever. As we did not have to worry about this life when we were still in the womb, so give us trust for our new life after death. **R**

Lord Jesus, you call us to be children of the Most High God, and to be good to those who wrong us. Help us love our enemies, pray for those who abuse us, and to love the loveless. **R**

All flesh knows pain and illness, and we continue to believe that you care about us, regardless of the health of our bodies. We pray for those who are weak in body, mind, or spirit: _____. **R**

Light of the world, shine upon us. **Amen.**

Texts: Genesis 45:3-11, 15   Psalm 37:1-11, 39-40   1 Corinthians 15:35-38, 42-50   Luke 6:27-38

8th Sunday after Epiphany

Responsive Sentence for the Sundays after Epiphany:
    Let us walk: **In the light of the Lord.**

Creator God, as you use sunshine and rain, soil and seed, to produce food for all your creatures, so your Word does not return to you empty. Ready our hearts to listen to your voice, and fill our hands with tasks that please you, that we may know the power of your Spirit. **R**

Make us glad, Holy Spirit, to be used by God. Hear our thanksgiving for the hope of producing the fruit of your Spirit, in song, in labor, through words and by deeds, inspired by your love. **R**

Mysterious Lord, you promise a great change in us from this world to the next. When that moment comes, when death is swallowed up in victory, and the trumpet sounds, and the dead are raised to eternal life, let our joy be great! **R**

Light of the World, Jesus Christ, you caution us to build a firm foundation in the faith, so that we will be able to stand in times of storm and misfortune. Teach us to become builders of trust, faith, hope and love. **R**

Though this world shall pass away, we rejoice that your powerful Word is forever. **R**

Living God, we bring before you people we know and love, remembering both the mystery of healing and the mystery of the resurrection to a new life. Care for all for whom we pray: _____. **R**

Light of the world, shine upon us. **Amen.**

Texts: Sirach 27:4-7 or Isaiah 55:10-13   Psalm 92:1-4, 12-15   1 Corinthians 15:51-58   Luke 6:39-49

YEAR C

Transfiguration of Our Lord

Responsive Sentence for the Transfiguration of Our Lord:
    Lord of the Transfiguration: **Change us by your Word.**

Heavenly Father, even as Moses' face shone after being in your presence, brighten our lives with the presence of Christ the Lord, that our hearts may burn with joy when we hear His Word. **R**

Holy God, lover of justice, let us receive your decrees and commands with serious faith, for it is your pleasure to guide us, forgive us, and make us accountable to your Word. **R**

Holy Spirit, never let us lose heart. Transform us into the image of Christ, as we engage in ministry. **R**

Lord Jesus, help us imagine being with you on the Mount of Transfiguration, hearing the voice of the Lord saying, "This is my Son, my Chosen; listen to Him!" **R**

God of all gods, removing the divinity of everything else we would follow, help us turn to you as the singular source of the Divine. **R**

Lord Jesus, even as you cast out demons, healed the sick, and raised the dead, we come before you with the needs of many, now named in your presence: _____. **R**

Light of the world, shine upon us. **Amen.**

Texts: Exodus 34:29-35   Psalm 99   2 Corinthians 3:12—4:2   Luke 9:28-36 [37-43]

Ash Wednesday

Responsive Sentence for Ash Wednesday:
 The day of the Lord is coming: **He abounds in steadfast love.**

Lord God Almighty, your prophets warn us to tremble at your coming, for it will be a day of darkness and gloom. They advise us to return to you with our hearts, so that our gloom may be turned into the noonday sun, for you are also gracious and merciful. **R**

Have mercy on us, O God, and blot out our sins. Against you and you alone have we sinned, for all our wrong against others is against a beloved child of your own. Create in us new hearts, and put a new and right spirit within us. **R**

Lord Jesus Christ, as fellow servants of God we may be treated as imposters, yet you make us true. We may be accused of being sorrowful, but we rejoice in your presence. We may be pitied because we are seen as poor and having nothing but faith, but you make us rich in the love of God. **R**

Holy Spirit, help us hear the words of Jesus as the Word of God. Help our hearts treasure your presence more than the treasures of the world. When we do find ourselves loving you above all else, help us to be humble in spirit, for it is your gift, not our accomplishment. **R**

We bring before you those who are well aware of their physical weaknesses, for they stand in need of your healing. As we name them aloud or silently in our hearts, help us remember again that we, too, are dust, and to dust we shall return: _____. **R**

Though we remember we are dust and to dust we shall return, we remember that we are your precious dust. **Amen.**

Texts: Joel 2:1-2, 12-17   Psalm 51:1-17   2 Corinthians 5:20b—6:10   Matthew 6:1-6, 16-21

1st Sunday in Lent

Responsive Sentence for the Sundays in Lent:
    In the day of trial: **Be present, Lord.**

Heavenly Father, you give us cause to celebrate because you deliver us like you delivered Israel from Egypt. Fill our hearts with thanksgiving for the mighty work of Jesus Christ for our salvation. **R**

Almighty God, you not only shelter us in our homes and churches, you provide angels to guard us. Help us cling to you, and call upon you, all the days of our lives. **R**

Holy Spirit, so near to us, enable us to confess with true conviction that Jesus is Lord. **R**

Jesus, full of the Holy Spirit, tempted by Satan in the wilderness to be something less than the Son of God, be with us when we are tempted to be something less than a child of God. **R**

Lord Jesus Christ, remember your temptations in the wilderness and understand our human weaknesses. Send your Holy Spirit to counsel and console us in the darker days of our faith. **R**

All the world groans in travail, Lord Jesus, and many suffer from heartbreak and disease. Hear us as we name those who need your healing help: _____. **R**

From every wilderness day, Good Lord deliver us. **Amen**.

Texts: Deuteronomy 26:1-11   Psalm 91:1-2, 9-16   Romans 10:8b-13   Luke 4:1-13

2nd Sunday in Lent

Responsive Sentence for the Sundays in Lent:
 In the day of trial: **Be present, Lord.**

Heavenly Father, your plans for us are more numerous than the stars of heaven, so great is your love. When we doubt, like Abraham, assure us of the dependability of your promises. **R**

Holy Spirit, when terrors approach us like nightmares, scatter our gloom and darkness until our hearts are able to seek your holy face. **R**

Lord God, you are our light and salvation. We ask above all else to live with you all the days of our lives. **R**

Lord Jesus Christ, able to transform our body of death into a citizen of heaven, help us live boldly in the way of the cross. **R**

Holy Spirit, gather us into the arms of Jesus, like a hen gathers her brood under her wings when the fox is near. By the strength of grace, grant us the power to pray, "Blessed is the one who comes in the name of the Lord." **R**

Hear us as we pray for those known to us suffering trials and in need of your nearness: _____. **R**

From every wilderness day, Good Lord deliver us. **Amen**.

Texts: Genesis 15:1-12, 17-18   Psalm 27   Philippians 3:17—4:1   Luke 13:31-35 or Luke 9:28-36

YEAR C

3rd Sunday in Lent

Responsive Sentence for the Sundays in Lent:
   In the day of trial: **Be present, Lord.**

Almighty God, your heavens and your ways are higher than our ideas, our hopes or our plans. Abundantly pardon us, that we may live a joyful life in the spirit of your love. **R**

Holy Spirit, when we cling to God with our whole being, remind us that God has an even tighter grip on us, and His right hand holds us fast. **R**

Lord Jesus Christ, tested in the wilderness, be with us when we feel tempted, and be our help in the day of trouble. **R**

Lord Jesus Christ, you call us to repentance, and you call us to produce fruit for the kingdom. Forgive us when we balk at witness and serving, forgetting the need to be obedient to the Way of the Cross. **R**

Holy Spirit, help us see Christ at work among us, at work by us and through us, and at work on us, that we may grow in the faith. **R**

Lord Jesus, we may not know that some of us need healing, because the disease is not yet obvious. Heal us all, with special attention to those whom we name aloud: _____. **R**

From every wilderness day, Good Lord deliver us. **Amen**.

Texts: Isaiah 55:1-9   Psalm 63:1-8   1 Corinthians 10:1-13   Luke 13:1-9

4th Sunday in Lent

Responsive Sentence for the Sundays in Lent:
    In the day of trial: **Be present, Lord.**

Heavenly Father, when our wilderness journey ends and normality returns to our lives, remind us to look back and see where you carried us through, deepened our faith, and provided us with your loving care. **R**

Holy Spirit, when suffering is the result of our own sin, inspire us to turn around, ask for help, accept your forgiveness, and live a new life in your grace. **R**

Holy Spirit, Reconciling God, in Christ make us a new creation, by forgiving our sins and sending us out with a mission to be your ambassadors of love, peace and new life. **R**

Almighty God, hope beyond hope, love beyond understanding, forgiver and forgetter of our awful sins, wait for us in patience, but needle us with the memory of your loving self, your loving home. **R**

Lord Jesus, as you told parables in order to make the gospel clear, put us in a story of your choosing, and bring us to a deeper faith in you. **R**

We pray for those who need to be reminded that there is healing in your presence, and homecoming, because there is a home: _____. **R**

From every wilderness day, Good Lord deliver us. **Amen**.

Texts: Joshua 5:9-12   Psalm 32   2 Corinthians 5:16-21   Luke 15:1-3, 11b-32

5th Sunday in Lent

Responsive Sentence for the Sundays in Lent:
    In the day of trial: **Be present, Lord.**

Almighty God, as you delivered your people from Egypt and Babylon, so lead us out of the wilderness of our confusion and doubt. **R**

Holy Spirit, hear our songs of praise and shouts of joy when we see our sufferings coming to an end and our losses restored, both in this world and the next. **R**

Holy Spirit, as the pains of the past diminish in our memory, give us courage to press on toward the prize of the heavenly call of God in Christ Jesus. **R**

Lord Jesus Christ, as you accept our gifts of love, no matter how simple or costly they are, defend us from those who would criticize our faithful generosity. **R**

As Martha and Mary served you at dinner and anointed your feet, so fill us with hospitality, that we may know the joy of being with you at table. **R**

The ill among us are named in love, Lord Jesus, that you might comfort and heal according to your most holy will: _____. **R**

From every wilderness day, Good Lord deliver us. **Amen**.

Texts: Isaiah 43:16-21   Psalm 126   Philippians 3:4b-14   John 12:1-8

6th Sunday in Lent
Sunday of the Passion, Palm Sunday

Responsive Sentence for the Sundays in Lent:
  In the day of trial: **Be present, Lord.**

Heavenly Father, our helper when we are weary, our protector from those who dislike us, may we listen to your morning call, and speak the truth in love. **R**

Holy Spirit, when we feel as useless as a broken pot, let your face shine upon us, that we may be restored. **R**

Lord Jesus, you know what life is like in human form, for you lived and died as one of us. Fill us with anticipation for the day when we rise from the dead to be alive in the Spirit forever. **R**

In your passion, Lord Jesus, you suffered from false accusations, painful lashings, thorns and nails. Lifted up on the cross you felt every human emotion possible. How great thou art to love like this for us. May we, like you, commit our spirits to God on the day of our dying, anticipating the glorious resurrection of the dead. **R**

In you mercy, hear us as we name those who are ill: _____. **R**

From every wilderness day, Good Lord deliver us. **Amen**.

Texts for the Liturgy of the Palms: Luke 19:28-40   Psalm 118:1-2, 19-29

Texts for the Liturgy of the Passion: Isaiah 50:4-9a   Psalm 31:9-16   Philippians 2:5-11   Luke 22:14—23:56 or Luke 23:1-49

YEAR C

Maundy Thursday

Responsive Sentence for Maundy Thursday:
    Let us love one another: **As Christ has loved us.**

Lord Jesus Christ, we often see Peter's reluctance to have you wash his feet as our hesitation in all things spiritual, for you end up touching the physical. You end up touching us. Give us the courage to let you touch us, head to toe. **R**

Lord Jesus Christ, you command us to wash each other's feet. The indignity never ends! Yet we know what to ask. Give us the courage to touch one another, for the sake of healing, head to toe. **R**

Holy Spirit, courage-giver, teach us how to bend our knees, fold our hands, and lift up our eyes to the loving Father, who cared so much that He sent us His Son to die for us. We cannot match the humiliation of Jesus, but we give thanks for His holy work on our behalf. **R**

Heavenly Father, you single us out for love of such depth and beauty that we can scarcely stand it, or understand it. For the love of us, you gave your only Son! **R**

Your new commandment, Lord Jesus, is to love one another as you have loved us. When you kneel before us, towel in hand, we know we are not worthy. Wash us anyway. Make us humble. Help us be each other's keeper. **R**

Though we remember we are dust and to dust we shall return, we remember that we are your precious dust. **Amen.**

Texts: Exodus 12:1-4 [5-10] 11-14   Psalm 116:1-2, 12-19   1 Corinthians 11:23-26   John 13:1-17, 31b-35

Good Friday

Responsive Sentence for Good Friday:
    God of the ages: **You love us.**

Heavenly Father, the pain of Good Friday is rebellion against you. You sent a Son, your one and only, and they crucified Him because all generations want a God unlike the God who is you. It is our sin to want you to be bold and brave, strong and militant, rather than a God filled with so much mercy and love. **R**

Holy Spirit, you were there in power, giving Jesus the will to die for the likes of us. We do not know what you whispered in His heart, or what you reminded Him of in His memory. We only know He did not stop the awful crucifixion, which was His alone to cancel. **R**

Lord Jesus Christ, we see ourselves in Pontius Pilate, your judge. He was trapped, like we are, dealing with you on this earth where justice so often means punishment. He did not know how to say "no" to death. **R**

Forgive us, Father, Son and Holy Spirit. We do not know all that we have done. It is not our ignorance which emboldens us to ask for forgiveness. It is your death, your love, your power and your mercy. And more than all of this, it is our desire to be with you forever. **R**

Into your hands we commend all who do not know you, but need you. Help us ache for their discovery of a God so good that He loves even those of us who walk away. **R**

Though we remember we are dust and to dust we shall return, we remember that we are your precious dust. **Amen.**

Texts: Isaiah 52:13—53:12   Psalm 22   Hebrews 10:16-25 or Hebrews 4:14-16; 5:7-9   John 18:1—19:42

Easter Day
Resurrection of Our Lord

Responsive Sentence for the Sundays of Easter:
  Come into our hearts, Lord Jesus: **Come into our hearts to stay.**

Almighty God, you show no partiality, but forgive the sins of all of us through the name of your Son, Jesus Christ. **R**

Heavenly Father, the special day that you have made for us is our Day of Resurrection. Let us rejoice and be glad in it. **R**

Holy Spirit, move us beyond hope for this day only, to the promise of a new life in Jesus Christ. Destroy death, our last enemy, for the kingdom of God is established. **R**

Lord Jesus Christ, destroyer of sin, death and the devil, take us under the rule of love, as we rejoice in your resurrection. **R**

Holy Spirit, what seemed like an idle tale to the men who heard the first report of the resurrection, you have verified again and again by Christ's presence among us. **R**

Turn the weeping of those who mourn the deaths of those whom they love into the joyful expectation of eternal life for all who belong to you. **R**

Christ lives with us. **Amen.**

Texts: Acts 10:34-43 or Isaiah 65:17-25   Psalm 118:1-2, 14-24   1 Corinthians 15:19-26 or Acts 10:34-43   John 20:1-18 or Luke 24:1-12

2nd Sunday of Easter

Responsive Sentence for the Sundays of Easter:
   Come into our hearts, Lord Jesus: **Come into our hearts to stay.**

Holy Spirit, as you gave courage and confidence to the disciples to proclaim the risen Christ, despite the warnings of the authorities, so let us be unflappable with the beauty, the power and the urgency of the gospel message. **R**

Help us look forward, Heavenly Father, to the day of resurrection as your gift of eternal life. **R**

Lord Jesus Christ, chief cornerstone of the church, build up our lives true to your will. **R**

Holy Spirit, as you inspired the prophets to see beyond the affairs of this earth, so inspire us with the eyes of faith to see the return of Christ as Our Savior. **R**

Lord Jesus Christ, when we are deep in doubt, open your wounded side to our touch, and let us see the print of the nails in your hands, that we may be restored to active discipleship in your name. **R**

Come now, Lord Jesus, with your healing power, and touch all of us who doubt, who are ill, and who need you very near: _____. **R**

Christ lives with us. **Amen.**

Texts: Acts 5:27-32   Psalm 118:14-29 or Psalm 150   Revelation 1:4-8   John 20:19-31

3rd Sunday of Easter

Responsive Sentence for the Sundays of Easter:
    Come into our hearts, Lord Jesus: **Come into our hearts to stay.**

Holy Spirit, shine the bright light of Jesus Christ upon us, like it happened to Saul on the road to Damascus, and let our new family name forever be known as "Christian." **R**

Lord Jesus Christ, give us the vision and faith of the Psalmists who know whom to thank for healing. **R**

Lamb of God, as on the cross you sacrificed yourself for us, so receive our gifts of prayer and praise as offerings of love for all that you have done for us. **R**

Lord Jesus Christ, when you returned to the shore of the sea where you first called Peter, you re-commissioned him to follow you. Revisit us with the same love that first won our hearts, that we may hear your commission to follow you all the days of our lives. **R**

Jesus Christ, you ask us to love you above all else, all others, even above our very selves. Help us commit our bodies and souls into your love and care. **R**

For those among us experiencing the frailty of this world's physical body, prolong, restore and heal, as you will, those who are ill: _____. **R**

Christ lives with us. **Amen.**

Texts: Acts 9:1-6 [7-20]   Psalm 30   Revelation 5:11-14   John 21:1-19

4th Sunday of Easter

Responsive Sentence for the Sundays of Easter:
Come into our hearts, Lord Jesus: **Come into our hearts to stay.**

Holy Spirit, fill us with faith to believe in the power of prayer, and give us courage to always prefer and accept your will over our own, in all that we might ask. **R**

Holy Spirit, full of the goodness and mercy of Jesus, our Good Shepherd, remind us that we are bound to live in the house of the Lord forever. **R**

Lord Jesus Christ, you passed through the great ordeal for us. When we pass through ordeals that are filled with uncertainty and pain, remind us of the God who will wipe away every tear from our eyes. **R**

Father God, one with Jesus the Christ, never allow us to forget or diminish your holy name, for we have been taught your name by your beloved Son. **R**

When all the world seems to be in conflict, Holy Spirit, remind us of the peace of God that passes understanding, and give us courage to relax and let God rule both the world and our turbulent hearts. **R**

We remember those in need who struggle for well being. Hear us as we call out their names: _____. **R**

Christ lives with us. **Amen.**

Texts: Acts 9:36-43   Psalm 23   Revelation 7:9-17   John 10:22-30

5th Sunday of Easter

Responsive Sentence for the Sundays of Easter:
    Come into our hearts, Lord Jesus: **Come into our hearts to stay.**

Holy Spirit, come to us like you came to the Gentiles, who accepted the word of God and repentance as a gift from God that leads to life. **R**

Holy Spirit, help us see the splendor of God over all that is on the earth and in the heavens above, that we may join the chorus of the universe in praise. **R**

Lord Jesus Christ, you make all things new, for you are the Alpha and the Omega, the beginning and the end, the Son of the Living God, who will wipe away all tears from all eyes. **R**

Lord Jesus, by example, you teach us to love one another, and you command us to love one another. Help us accept and obey your command as yet another gift of love. **R**

God of all people, help us rejoice in the vision you have of the family of God, for you include even us. **R**

Lord Jesus, hear us as we pray for the people in our minds and hearts who are in need: _____. **R**

Christ lives with us. **Amen.**

Texts: Acts 11:1-18   Psalm 148   Revelation 21:1-6   John 13:31-35

6th Sunday of Easter

Responsive Sentence for the Sundays of Easter:
Come into our hearts, Lord Jesus: **Come into our hearts to stay.**

Guide us, Holy Spirit, to seek places of worship to pray, sing, and to hear the gospel from those called to teach and preach. **R**

Almighty God, as the earth you created brings forth its food, medicines, and beauty, we stand in awe of you, and give you our thanksgiving. **R**

God Almighty, light of heaven; Lord Jesus Christ, the Lamb and the lamp of heaven, help us cling to your vision of a life with no more dark nights, where you reign with the Holy Spirit forever. **R**

Holy Spirit, continue to open our ears to the words of Jesus, who credits God the Father with all He teaches, and with all He does in love. **R**

Give us your peace, Lord Jesus, so that fear in our lives dissipates like fog. Hear our glad song as you celebrate your homecoming with Our Father. **R**

Lord Jesus, present in this world and in the world to come, care for those among us who struggle with problems, loneliness and disease: _____. **R**

Christ lives with us. **Amen.**

Texts: Acts 16:9-15   Psalm 67   Revelation 21:10, 22—22:5   John 14:23-29 or John 5:1-9

YEAR C

7th Sunday of Easter

Responsive Sentence for the Sundays of Easter:
   Come into our hearts, Lord Jesus: **Come into our hearts to stay.**

Holy Spirit, active behind prison doors, guard the saints who suffer for the faith, protect the innocent and arrange for their release, and be with all prisoners, that they may hear the message of your presence and love. **R**

Guard the lives of your saints, O Lord, and rescue us from the hands of the wicked, that we may know the light and joy of the only god, who is God. **R**

Come, Lord Jesus, into our every day, at our every meal, through our every illness, by our side, morning, noon and night. **R**

Lord Jesus, when you pray for us to the Father, (and we listen in), you fill us with expectation to be with you and to know the love of God that has been present since the foundation of the world. **R**

Lord Jesus, intimate with the Father, you have asked the Father that His love may also be in us. For making His name known to us, we give you thanks. **R**

In confidence that you are listening, Lord Jesus and Master Healer, hear our prayers for persons in need: _____. **R**

Christ lives with us. **Amen.**

Texts: Acts 16:16-34   Psalm 97   Revelation 22:12-14, 16-17, 20-21   John 17:20-26

The Day of Pentecost

Responsive Sentence for the Day of Pentecost:
    We come to you empty: **Fill us with your loving Spirit.**

Pour out your Spirit upon us, Lord God, and give us no fear of visions and dreams, of omens and signs, for these simply testify to the great and glorious day of your return in glory. **R**

Holy God, Creator of the universe, as you can snuff out a volcano with a touch and still the raging sea with a whisper, so quiet the roaring storm within us when we are lonely, in doubt or despair, and need your powerful gentle peace. **R**

As your children, "Abba! Father!", remind us of our adoption in baptism, and of our sisters and brothers in the family of faith that belongs to God. **R**

Holy Advocate, sent by the Father, remind us of Jesus whenever we fret or wonder about the Way of God. **R**

Loving Jesus, as the Father is in you, and you are in the Father, gather us by your Holy Spirit that we may be embraced in love by the Triune God. **R**

God of all mercies, we give you thanks for caring about untimely death and disease. Remind us of your time beyond time, and of your power to heal, as we name persons we know who are in need: _____. **R**

Loving God, you are true Love. **Amen.**

Texts: Acts 2:1-21 or Genesis 11:1-9   Psalm 104:24-34, 35b   Romans 8:14-17 or Acts 2:1-21   John 14:8-17 [25-27]

The Holy Trinity
First Sunday after Pentecost

Responsive Sentence for the Holy Trinity:
    Holy Trinity, One God: **You are our God.**

Creator God, Creator of Wisdom, your very first created partner in forming the earth and human beings, let us marvel at your work as scientists seek to discover the mysteries of the body, the earth and the universe. **R**

With our eyes, Lord God, we rejoice that we are part of your creative work. With all our senses we see you in this world and in the world beyond the physical. We give you thanks for creating us in your image, and visiting us with your love. **R**

Holy Spirit, as you pour hope into our hearts, help us receive it in joy, knowing it is God's love. **R**

Father, Son and Holy Spirit, you are one God coming to us in manifold ways. Be our guide, our truth, our chief love. **R**

As we seek to understand the mystery of the Holy Trinity, Lord God, you remind us that mysteries are mysteries for a reason. Therefore, though our understanding is limited, fill us with faith to believe and live as your person, today and always. **R**

We remember the joy of good health, and the pain of illness, and ask that you will use your power to heal those whom we name before you: _____. **R**

You are always with us, past the end of time. **Amen.**

Texts: Proverbs 8:1-4, 22-31   Psalm 8   Romans 5:1-5   John 16:12-15

Time after Pentecost, Lectionary 8C

Responsive Sentence for the Sundays after Pentecost:
    Loving Christ: **Help us share the faith.**

Heavenly Father, your holy word, spoken by prophets, priests, psalmists and people like us, is a power of magnificence and grace. We rejoice in the promise that your word never returns to you empty. **R**

Lord of Eternity, beyond space and time, you make our every morning, noon, and night worthy of praise. As we sing, hum, whistle or speak to you, we hope to make you glad. **R**

Death, our great enemy, is no match for you, Lord God. You are able to undo all the power of the evil one, and we commit ourselves into your loving care. **R**

Holy Spirit, you call us into the membership of the Body of Christ. Give us confidence that we will rise alive in the church triumphant, where our lives will be an eternal joy. **R**

Lord Jesus Christ, the seasons of our lives are all growing seasons for us, when we trust you for the morrow. As we name the people you've given us to love, we know you love them too: _____. **R**

Listening God, hear our prayers. **Amen.**

Texts: Sirach 27:4-7 or Isaiah 55:10-13   Psalm 92:1-4, 12-15   1 Corinthians 15:51-58   Luke 6:39-49

Dates: May 24 – May 28

YEAR C

Time after Pentecost, Lectionary 9C

Responsive Sentence for the Sundays after Pentecost:
    Loving Christ: **Help us share the faith.**

Heavenly Father, give us a sense of hospitality to those who do not know that you are the only God. When they call upon you, and you hear them in heaven, bring them to know that they are welcomed in this place where your name is known and spoken aloud. **R**

When false gods are worshiped around us, remind us, Holy Spirit, never to turn our backs upon the only God who is God. **R**

Righteous God, when you judge the people with your truth, remember we are created in your image, after your likeness. Above all, when you judge us, remember the love of Jesus for us. **R**

Lord Jesus Christ, even as you revealed the gospel to Paul, so reveal to us the never-ending love of God for the whole world. **R**

Holy Spirit, increase our faith by the reading of the Word, the hearing of the gospel, and the deliberate recollection of all the times you walked and talked with us. **R**

Lord Jesus, you have authority over death and disease, so we bring before you the names of those whom we commit to your care: _____. **R**

Listening God, hear our prayers. **Amen.**

Texts: 1 Kings 8:22-23, 41-43 or 1 Kings 18:20-21 [22-29] 30-39   Psalm 96:1-9 or Psalm 96   Galatians 1:1-12   Luke 7:1-10

Dates: May 29 – June 4

Time after Pentecost, Lectionary 10C

Responsive Sentence for the Sundays after Pentecost:
Loving Christ: **Help us share the faith.**

Heavenly Father, when we pray with passion like Elijah, you hear our faith at work. Listen to our perceived needs, but do what is really best for us. **R**

Holy Spirit, when you hear us sing praise to God, you know we have a healthy faith. Care also for our bodies when they are in need of repair and healing. **R**

Lord Jesus Christ, great teacher, preacher and healer, your greatest gift to us is the gospel of salvation, revealed to saints and sinners as the most loving act of God possible. **R**

Jesus, when you raised the widow's son from death, you gave us a glimpse of what you plan for each of us. Let us expect our resurrection with even greater joy, for it is the resurrection to eternal life. **R**

Lord God Almighty, remember the needs of those who till the soil, plant the seed, cut the wheat and feed the poor. We thank you for our daily bread. **R**

Lord Jesus Christ, healer and miracle worker, we know you can do all things, even for those with little faith. Now hear our prayers for those who need the benefit of your touch: _____. **R**

Listening God, hear our prayers. **Amen.**

Texts: 1 Kings 17:17-24 or 1 Kings 17:8-16 [17-24]   Psalm 30 or Psalm 146   Galatians 1:11-24   Luke 7:11-17

Dates: June 5 – June 11

Time after Pentecost, Lectionary 11C

Responsive Sentence for the Sundays after Pentecost:
    Loving Christ: **Help us share the faith.**

Heavenly Father, you loved David despite his awful sin and guilt. When we bear the consequences of sin, help us remember that your love is never diminished. **R**

Holy Spirit, when we suppose we have little to confess, forgive our ignorance. Turn us to trust you with our hearts, that we may learn both the joy and the pain of forgiving . . . and being forgiven. **R**

Lord Jesus Christ, grace giver, you justify us through faith in your work on the cross. By your Holy Spirit, give us a holy dependence upon you, that we might live a life worthy of your loving call. **R**

Lord Jesus, forgiver of sins, you take away the penalty of eternal death. Make our hearts glad to hear the gospel of eternal life, given to us as your gift of forgiving love from the cross. **R**

All the world, Heavenly Father, seems to be in conflict. Remove from us the despair we feel, so that we may live knowing that all that is to come is always under your review and correction. **R**

Lord Jesus Christ, forgiver and healer, let the power of your love touch those for whom we pray: _____. **R**

Listening God, hear our prayers. **Amen.**

Texts: 2 Samuel 11:26—12:10, 13-15 or 1 Kings 21:1-10 [11-14] 15-21a   Psalm 32 or Psalm 5:1-8   Galatians 2:15-21 Luke 7:36—8:3

Dates: June 12 – June 18

Time after Pentecost, Lectionary 12C

Responsive Sentence for the Sundays after Pentecost:
    Loving Christ: **Help us share the faith.**

Heavenly Father, keep your church from recreating you in images of the human self, for you alone are the holy one, and you forbid idolatry. **R**

Heavenly Father, when we look for you in the fearful earthquake, wind and fire, you come to us instead in silence, that we may know that we are never alone. **R**

Help us care for the hungry in their weakness, the poor in their need, and the rich in their many temptations. **R**

Holy Spirit, as you come us to in Holy Baptism, making us an heir of Abraham, help us live the promise that we belong to Jesus. **R**

Lord Jesus Christ, even as you cast out demons from those visited by evil, so purify our lives that we may give a clear witness to others of all that you have done in the shaping of our lives. **R**

Holy Spirit, gives us the willpower to say no to those habits of the day that disrupt the joy of being with you. Hear us, Lord Jesus, as we name those in need of your close company: _____. **R**

Listening God, hear our prayers. **Amen.**

Texts: Isaiah 65:1-9 or 1 Kings 19:1-4 [5-7] 8-15a   Psalm 22:19-28 or Psalms 42 and 43   Galatians 3:23-29   Luke 8:26-39

Dates: June 19 – June 25

Time after Pentecost, Lectionary 13C

Responsive Sentence for the Sundays after Pentecost:
    Loving Christ: **Help us share the faith.**

As the generations rise and fall before you, Heavenly Father, you provide persons of faith to continue your holy work on earth. We ask to be included among the faithful, that in our time, others will come to know your name, and serve you above all else. **R**

Give us a vision of the future, Holy Spirit, that we may sing like a Psalmist in confidence of a bright future with you in the world to come. **R**

Holy Spirit, let us live by your Spirit of love, joy, peace, patience, kindness, generosity, faithfulness, gentleness, and self-control above all other goals. **R**

Lord Jesus Christ, give us the will to be your faithful servants, and the help of the Holy Spirit for courage on the journey. **R**

Lord Jesus, resolute to go to Jerusalem to complete the tasks required for our redemption, receive our praise for your willingness to suffer and die for us. You, alone, make us fit for the kingdom of God. **R**

Great Physician, you know our infirmities before we even name a name. Yet we are bold to call upon you for those in need: _____. **R**

Listening God, hear our prayers. **Amen.**

Texts: 1 Kings 19:15-16, 19-21 or 2 Kings 2:1-2, 6-14   Psalm 16 or Psalm 77:1-2, 11-20   Galatians 5:1, 13-25   Luke 9:51-62

Dates: June 26 – July 2

Time after Pentecost, Lectionary 14C

Responsive Sentence for the Sundays after Pentecost:
    Loving Christ: **Help us share the faith.**

Lord God, as you comforted the returning exiles like a mother comforts her child, so encourage and embrace us in the changes that come upon us. **R**

Heavenly Father, like Naaman the leper who wanted a dramatic cure, we often want things fixed our way. As you humbled Naaman, and thus gave him a double cure, so care for us both in body and soul, according to your Word. **R**

Awesome God, keeping faith with us and providing all we need, we give you thanks for this life and for all the people given for us to love. **R**

Lord Jesus, keep us from growing weary in the faith as we wait for the harvest of souls to eternal life. **R**

Holy Spirit, fill us with joy that our names are written in heaven, for by grace we have been saved. **R**

Your mercies, Lord God, continue to be known by persons of faith. Now we ask you to care for those who need help beyond our ability to provide: _____. **R**

Listening God, hear our prayers. **Amen.**

Texts: Isaiah 66:10-14 or 2 Kings 5:1-14   Psalm 66:1-9 or Psalm 30   Galatians 6:[1-6] 7-16   Luke 10:1-11, 16-20

Dates: July 3 – July 9

Time after Pentecost, Lectionary 15C

Responsive Sentence for the Sundays after Pentecost:
   Loving Christ: **Help us share the faith.**

Lord God Almighty, your covenant with us requires obedience. Help us enjoy your Word, knowing that it is neither distant nor hard to grasp, for you have lovingly placed it into our hearts. **R**

Heavenly Father, open our ears and our hearts to see your love for all the world, that we may share your Word and care about your children in every land. **R**

Holy Spirit, as we learn to love mercy and to trust justice, remind us to care for both because we are children of the Most High God. **R**

Lord Jesus, as we seek to love God and our neighbors as ourselves, help us love with bold courage and sacrificial deeds. **R**

Heavenly Father, as you make the seasons change throughout the year, remind us of your constant love for all, regardless of the season of our lives. **R**

Great Physician, we care for those we lovingly bring before you, knowing that you will do what is best for all: _____. **R**

Listening God, hear our prayers. **Amen.**

Texts: Deuteronomy 30:9-14 or Amos 7:7-17   Psalm 25:1-10 or Psalm 82   Colossians 1:1-14   Luke 10:25-37

Dates: July 10 – July 16

Time after Pentecost, Lectionary 16C

Responsive Sentence for the Sundays after Pentecost:
    Loving Christ: **Help us share the faith.**

Lord God Almighty, as Abraham and Sarah extended the gift of hospitality to visiting strangers, open our hearts to share with others, and graciously receive the fulfillment of your promises. **R**

Holy Spirit, Lord God, as we run from new idea to strange idea, looking in vain for you, give us eyes to see you present, as you always are, in the form of the poor, the needy, and the hopeless. **R**

Heavenly Father, creator of visible things, and creator of invisible things, give us courage to trust you with this day, with tomorrow, and with our redemption to eternal life. **R**

Lord Jesus, the purity of your heart is obvious in the single desire to do the Father's will, at all times, in all places and at any cost. Help us keep our eyes focused on you as the singular Lord of our life. **R**

Holy Spirit, inspire us to see Christ alive in our very own lives. **R**

Lord Jesus Christ, Great Physician, remember us who are still in the earthly body, so that disease may be cured. We name those who need your healing power: _____. **R**

Listening God, hear our prayers. **Amen.**

Texts: Genesis 18:1-10a or Amos 8:1-12   Psalm 15 or Psalm 52   Colossians 1:15-28   Luke 10:38-42

Dates: July 17 – July 23

Time after Pentecost, Lectionary 17C

Responsive Sentence for the Sundays after Pentecost:
    Loving Christ: **Help us share the faith.**

Heavenly Father, as Abraham made intercession for those in danger of destruction because of their sin, hear our prayers for those who do not know your Word, believe in your Holy Spirit, or trust in your Son as the Way, the Truth and the Life. **R**

Holy Spirit, convert those who do not care that you care for them, that all may become children of the living God. **R**

Lord God, ever working to create a world of love active in faith, do not abandon the work of your hands, nor the sacrifice of Jesus for our sin, for He is very dear to us, and we are very dear to Him. **R**

Lord Jesus, though the world is seldom aware of the great salvation drama happening among all who have been created in the image of God, give us a sense of urgency to proclaim your Lordship. **R**

Holy Spirit, keep us from being lured into false teaching, fancy new gods, or causes that compromise the faith delivered to the saints. **R**

Lord Jesus Christ, Bread of Life, even as you taught us to pray to Our Father for our daily bread, hear our prayer for your presence in our Holy Communion. **R**

Holy Spirit, we ask for you to come into our lives. We knock on every door trusting that you will open the right ones for us. We search for you in the daily events of our lives. Give us the good gift of your presence. **R**

We call upon you, Lord Jesus, to tend to those who need healing among us: _____. **R**

Listening God, hear our prayers. **Amen.**

Texts: Genesis 18:20-32 or Hosea 1:2-10   Psalm 138 or Psalm 85   Colossians 2:6-15 [16-19]   Luke 11:1-13

Dates: July 24 – July 30

Time after Pentecost, Lectionary 18C

Responsive Sentence for the Sundays after Pentecost:
    Loving Christ: **Help us share the faith.**

Lord God, when we sense that all that we do in this world is either in vain, or is vanity itself, remind us of the world to come, with your loving Son, and an eternity beyond the physical. **R**

Heavenly Father, even as you would not let Israel disappear into oblivion, so rescue and restore us to the Love that will never let us go. **R**

Holy Spirit, wisdom and wealth will perish like wickedness, but you endure beyond all graves. So incline our ears to listen to the one who was able to ransom us from futility and death, even Jesus Christ, our Lord. **R**

Lord Jesus Christ, give us the will to let go of everything that interferes with our love for the things are from above. **R**

Holy Spirit, always reminding us of the riches of God that far surpass the pleasures of this world, help us remember: "Thy kingdom comes." **R**

We struggle, Lord Jesus, with heavy feet planted in this world's values, needs and desires. Lift up our eyes, that we may see the world without an end. **R**

As we struggle with tragedy, death, sorrow, pain and fear, come Lord Jesus, rescue us from losses that injure our hope and faith. Hear our prayers for those in need: _____. **R**

Listening God, hear our prayers. **Amen.**

Texts: Ecclesiastes 1:2, 12-14; 2:18-23 or Hosea 11:1-11   Psalm 49:1-12 or Psalm 107:1-9, 43   Colossians 3:1-11   Luke 12:13-21

Dates: July 31 – August 6

YEAR C

Time after Pentecost, Lectionary 19C

Responsive Sentence for the Sundays after Pentecost:
    Loving Christ: **Help us share the faith.**

Heavenly Father, Creator of the universe, when we doubt send us out, like Abraham, to count the stars at night, and marvel at your might. **R**

Holy Spirit, help us learn to do good, seek justice, rescue the oppressed, defend the orphan, plead for the widow and worship you by deed, as well as by voice. **R**

Your loving kindness, Great God Almighty, is upon us, so let our expectations of goodness from you soar. **R**

Lord Jesus, make our faith strong so we may be filled with the assurance of countless good things coming, yet unseen, prepared by God for all of us. **R**

Lord Jesus, we look forward to your return at the unexpected hour, and we ask for the Holy Spirit to help us live lives of generosity and love. **R**

Great Physician, as we name those who need your loving care, help them sense your healing touch: _____. **R**

Listening God, hear our prayers. **Amen.**

Texts: Genesis 15:1-6 or Isaiah 1:1, 10-20   Psalm 33:12-22 or Psalm 50:1-8, 22-23   Hebrews 11:1-3, 8-16 Luke 12:32-40

Dates: August 7 – August 13

Time after Pentecost, Lectionary 20C

Responsive Sentence for the Sundays after Pentecost:
    Loving Christ: **Help us share the faith.**

Heavenly Father, protect us from false prophets who report their dreams, but not your Word. When you speak with fierce power, help us repent and faithfully follow your command. **R**

Holy Spirit, you have cultivated your church with holy care. Now, keep us from bearing worthless fruit, for your expectations of us demand our best. **R**

Lord God Almighty, you give us life, care for us, and often see us turn away from you. Bring us back, for without you we have no purpose, no goal, and love only for ourselves. **R**

Strong God, you parted the Red Sea, made the walls of Jericho fall, and have provided us with a great number of witnesses to your might. Help us run the race of perseverance you have given each of us to run, keeping our eyes only on you. **R**

Lord Jesus Christ, you felt the pressure of the looming death you had to die for us. When the stresses of this life are upon us, help us bear our cross like one bound to win, for you are with us. **R**

Lord Jesus, you know about our family and friends who are sick, injured, lonely, frustrated and often empty of hope. Hear us as we name them in love, and visit each, as only you can do: _____. **R**

Listening God, hear our prayers. **Amen.**

Texts: Jeremiah 23:23-29 or Isaiah 5:1-7   Psalm 82 or Psalm 80:1-2, 8-19   Hebrews 11:29—12:2   Luke 12:49-56

Dates: August 14 – August 20

Time after Pentecost, Lectionary 21C

Responsive Sentence for the Sundays after Pentecost:
  Loving Christ: **Help us share the faith.**

Heavenly Father, help us delight in worship on every sabbath day, for you delight to hear us sing, pray, and give you thanks together. **R**

Holy Spirit, remind us that you had plans for us before we were born, and like Jeremiah, regardless of our age, please use us well. **R**

Heavenly Father, forgiver of sins, healer of disease, giver of opportunities to be your person in the most surprising ways, we bless your holy name. **R**

God Almighty, you have been known as a consuming fire, but now you come as the God who shakes away created things, so that holy things, which cannot be shaken away, remain. Receive our reverence and our awe as our worship. **R**

Lord Jesus Christ, you have made the Sabbath Day holier than ever, by healing another. As part of our worship, help us reach out to others on this day of worship. **R**

You know of more needs among us than we know, Lord Jesus. Nevertheless, we name persons who wish you near, and ask for your healing: _____. **R**

Listening God, hear our prayers. **Amen.**

Texts: Isaiah 58:9b-14 or Jeremiah 1:4-10   Psalm 103:1-8 or Psalm 71:1-6   Hebrews 12:18-29   Luke 13:10-17

Dates: August 21 – August 27

Time after Pentecost, Lectionary 22C

Responsive Sentence for the Sundays after Pentecost:
    Loving Christ: **Help us share the faith.**

Heavenly Father, you remind us to consider humility as a virtue. Help us live our lives in the shadow of Christ our Lord, who was humble, even to death on the cross. **R**

Holy Spirit, keep us from repeating the mistakes of our ancestors who forsook you, even after you led them through the wilderness. **R**

Holy Spirit, we thank you for the witness of ancestors who gave freely to the poor, while their selfish neighbors lived only for themselves. Honor us with opportunities to be generous. **R**

Lord Jesus Christ, shape our lives with your love. **R**

Lord Jesus Christ, you make us imagine the poor sitting at our supper tables with the rest of our family, for all of us are children of God. Give us courage to move beyond imagination to real fellowship with those in need. **R**

Hear us as we name those among us in need of your special attention and loving care: _____. **R**

Listening God, hear our prayers. **Amen.**

Texts: Sirach 10:12-18 or Proverbs 25:6-7 or Jeremiah 2:4-13   Psalm 112 or Psalm 81:1, 10-16   Hebrews 13:1-8, 15-16 Luke 14:1, 7-14

Dates: August 28 – September 3

Time after Pentecost, Lectionary 23C

Responsive Sentence for the Sundays after Pentecost:
> Loving Christ: **Help us share the faith.**

Lord God, help us in our choices to serve you and you alone. Forbid that we would seek a lesser god. Help us understand that you permit no one but you as Lord and Master of our souls. **R**

Heavenly Father, we are clay in your hands. You took us from the earth and made us real human beings, made in your likeness, after your image. Use us as you see fit. **R**

Holy Spirit, you despise the light chaff which the wind drives away, because we were created in the solid image of God. Help us walk in the counsel of the Lord. **R**

Holy Spirit, as we try to walk in the path of the Lord, remind us that we were knit together, by you, in our mother's womb, and you claim us as your own creation. **R**

Lord Jesus Christ, you require an allegiance way beyond our imagination. Unless you help us carry the cross, we cannot bear the cost of discipleship. We give you what we can, trusting in your mercy to forgive our lack of total surrender. **R**

Lord Jesus Christ, we pray that you will accept our meager response to your hard commands. Remember, we are but facsimiles of your holy image. **R**

We name before you those in need of healing. We know each of them by name, as do you, but you, alone, are the Great Physician: _____. **R**

Listening God, hear our prayers. **Amen.**

Texts; Deuteronomy 30:15-20 or Jeremiah 18:1-11   Psalm 1 or Psalm 139:1-6, 13-18   Philemon 1-21   Luke 14:25-33

Dates: September 4 – September 10

Time after Pentecost, Lectionary 24C

Responsive Sentence for the Sundays after Pentecost:
    Loving Christ: **Help us share the faith.**

Heavenly Father, remember Isaac, Abraham, Israel and each of us as your faithful descendants, and help us obey your command to love. **R**

Lord God Almighty, help us understand your hard commands against sin. We know you do not tolerate foolishness, evil, nonsense or ignorance, for you are not deceived. Spare us from our false hope of mercy when we continue in our sin and hide behind your goodness. **R**

Holy Spirit, when we sin against one another, it is a sin against you. Help us confess our wrongdoing, and seek forgiveness, for the sake of righteousness, and for the sake of peace. **R**

Lord God, you alone are our refuge. Look down upon us and forgive us when we think that there is no God watching us. **R**

Lord Jesus Christ, give us the faith of Timothy who knew he was the chief of all sinners, but committed his heart, love and soul to you despite his weaknesses. **R**

Lord Jesus Christ, you rejoice when we repent. Help us admit our sin, receive your forgiveness, and begin again as children of the Heavenly Father. **R**

Merciful God, healer of our every ill, we bring before you by name those who need you near: _____. **R**

Listening God, hear our prayers. **Amen.**

Texts: Exodus 32:7-14 or Jeremiah 4:11-12, 22-28   Psalm 51:1-10 or Psalm 14   1 Timothy 1:12-17
Luke 15:1-10

Dates: September 11 – September 17

Time after Pentecost, Lectionary 25C

Responsive Sentence for the Sundays after Pentecost:
    Loving Christ: **Help us share the faith.**

Lord God Almighty, you know our desire for ease and well-being. Help us look up from our table of plenty to see those in need of bread for the day. **R**

Heavenly Father, you let us own property for our time on earth, as a trust and as a sign of your presence among us. We give you thanks for entrusting us to be stewards of all that you have created. **R**

Lord God, your holy wings hover over us and your faithfulness rises like the sun. You are our defense against the night, the arrows of the thief, and the plagues of the ruthless. Receive our thanksgiving for your protection. **R**

Holy Spirit, keep us from believing that security comes from wealth. You, Lord, are our only hope, our guide in the day of darkness, and our deliverance on our day of departing, all for which we give you our thanksgiving. **R**

Lord Jesus, help us see the poor, visit the poor, and care for them as our sisters and brothers in need. **R**

We remember those in distress of body, mind and spirit, and bring them before you in prayer: _____. **R**

Listening God, hear our prayers. **Amen.**

Texts: Amos 8:4-7 or Jeremiah 8:18—9:1   Psalm 113 or Psalm 79:1-9   1 Timothy 2:1-7   Luke 16:1-13

Dates: September 18 – September 24

Time after Pentecost, Lectionary 26C

Responsive Sentence for the Sundays after Pentecost:
    Loving Christ: **Help us share the faith.**

Heavenly Father, as your prophet, Amos, sternly reminded the Israelites to share their wealth with the poor, receive our gifts as signs of our recognition that all our good things have come from you to share. **R**

Lord God Almighty, as your prophet, Jeremiah, purchased land in Israel as a sign of hope that the exile was ending, so let our actions reflect our expectations that you will renew and restore your people, wherever they long to live. **R**

Holy Spirit, even as the Lord cares for the stranger and those in need of family, so help us in the sharing of ourselves, our homes and our possessions. **R**

Holy Spirit, you remind us that the love of money is the root of all evil, for it traps us with desires apart from those in need. Help us learn the joy of giving for the sake of others. **R**

Lord Jesus Christ, give us courage not only to share our wealth with the less fortunate, but to see the unfortunate one as our beloved brother or sister, and a child of your own redeeming. **R**

Holy Spirit, open our eyes to see the needs that are hard to notice when all is well with us, and when we notice the need of another, compel us to help. **R**

That all may know care inspired by love, Lord Jesus, we ask you to visit the ill among us: _____. **R**

Listening God, hear our prayers. **Amen.**

Texts: Amos 6:1a, 4-7 or Jeremiah 32:1-3a, 6-15   Psalm 146 or Psalm 91:1-6, 14-16   1 Timothy 6:6-19   Luke 16:19-31

Dates: September 25 – October 1

YEAR C

Time after Pentecost, Lectionary 27C

Responsive Sentence for the Sundays after Pentecost:
　　Loving Christ:　　　　　　　　　　**Help us share the faith.**

Lord God Almighty, you hear the complaints of those who see never-ending cruel injustice. Remind us that evil will end, and that the righteous live by faith alone. **R**

Holy Spirit, even as tears streak the cheeks of the one who grieves, so comfort all who are exiled or uprooted from homes they love, through storm, war, fire or foreclosure. **R**

Holy Spirit, your Psalmist reminds us to refrain from anger and rage, for it leads to evil. Give us patience whenever we are wronged, that we may not react in a way that makes a problem worse. **R**

Lord Jesus Christ, even as faith comes alive in us as your gift of the Holy Spirit, grant that we may joyfully use your gift of a living faith in our daily lives. **R**

Lord Jesus, Master, when we ask you to "Increase our faith," you tell us to serve others and to expect no thank-you or reward. Help us live as though we are available to God for any reason, at any time. Master, help us live as your worthy slaves. **R**

Holy Spirit, the world in its need, and sometimes in its greed, is always ready to be served. Help us serve you first, others second, and seek to live as obedient servants, always listening for your call. **R**

We bring before you, Lord Jesus, those with physical needs, in spiritual crisis, or mental anguish. Hear us as we name persons in need of prayer:_____. **R**

Listening God, hear our prayers. **Amen.**

Texts:　Habakkuk 1:1-4; 2:1-4 or Lamentations 1:1-6　Psalm 37:1-9 or Lamentations 3:19-26 or Psalm 137
2 Timothy 1:1-14　Luke 17:5-10

Dates:　October 2 – October 8

Time after Pentecost, Lectionary 28C

Responsive Sentence for the Sundays after Pentecost:
  Loving Christ: **Help us share the faith.**

Heavenly Father, when you provided for the healing of Naaman through your prophet Elisha, you healed more than his leprosy. When we ask you for healing, heal our bodies, our broken spirits, and our weakened faith, that we may be more fully yours, now and forever. **R**

Holy Spirit, great are your works, your majesty, and your persuasion. Give us a trust in the Lord, that our praises may be joyful, true and sure. **R**

Jesus Christ, you are "risen from the dead." That is the good news, the gospel. As we seek to be your workers in this world, help us both give and receive encouragement from one another. **R**

We thank you, Holy Spirit, for all the workers in the church, the ordained, the laity, and especially those so unnoticed and seldom thanked. **R**

Lord Jesus Christ, thank you. Thank you for healing every one of us in this place today. Thank you for spending miracles on us. Thank you for reminding us whom to thank for every blessing. **R**

Lord Jesus Christ, as receivers of your mercy throughout the years, hear us pray for others in distress, even as we name them aloud in prayer: _____. **R**

Listening God, hear our prayers. **Amen.**

Texts: 2 Kings 5:1-3, 7-15c or Jeremiah 29:1, 4-7   Psalm 111 or Psalm 66:1-12   2 Timothy 2:8-15
Luke 17:11-19

Dates: October 9 – October 15

Time after Pentecost, Lectionary 29C

Responsive Sentence for the Sundays after Pentecost:
    Loving Christ: **Help us share the faith.**

Heavenly Father, when we wrestle with you like Jacob did, you wrestle back. As we seek to know you and love you by your given name, bless us, for you are unlike every other person in our lives. **R**

Almighty God, write your covenant on our hearts with the certainty of your love, no matter how far we wander away. The seal of your good promise for us is forgiveness, a new life, a holy walk with you and with your saints of today. **R**

Holy Spirit, watch over us like a mother with her new born child, for we need you every hour. **R**

Holy Spirit, as we seek to observe the commandments of God written on our hearts, make your words as sweet as honey, your ways a daily delight. **R**

Lord God Almighty, guide the preachers of your Word, that all may speak with sound doctrine, based on the Holy Scriptures. **R**

Lord Jesus Christ, help us pray always and never lose heart. And if we do lose heart, restore us quickly with an outpouring of your love. **R**

Out of love for others, hear us name those in need of healing, that they may know you care for them like an only child: _____. **R**

Listening God, hear our prayers. **Amen.**

Texts: Genesis 32:22-31 or Jeremiah 31:27-34   Psalm 121 or Psalm 119:97-104   2 Timothy 3:14—4:5   Luke 18:1-8

Dates: October 16 – October 22

Time after Pentecost, Lectionary 30C

Responsive Sentence for the Sundays after Pentecost:
   Loving Christ: **Help us share the faith.**

Heavenly Father, forgive us when we fail to come to you in prayer when rain is scarce, peace is absent, and troubled times prevail. Yet you are among us, we are still called by your name, so we ask for your help for the sake of our nation and the world. **R**

Lord God, our only God, you call us your children even while we forget to rejoice and give thanks for all your gifts. Pour out your spirit among us in such abundance that our children will care about your Word, believe you are still active among us, and have a plan greater than human imaginations can fathom. **R**

Holy Spirit, make of us your pilgrim people, willing to walk a new road with you. Remind us that we are always in the presence of the God who cares about our journey. **R**

Lord Jesus Christ, give us the joy of St. Paul, who when facing death was able to say, "I have fought the good fight, I have finished the race, I have kept the faith." **R**

Lord Jesus Christ, let none of us boast about our goodness, for we know that we have all fallen far short of perfection. We know we need your mercy, and we believe that you will give it to us out of love. **R**

As we are able to love one another on earth, and feel the pains of those who need healing, be the Great Physician for those whom we name before you: _____. **R**

Listening God, hear our prayers. **Amen.**

Texts: Sirach 35:12-17 or Jeremiah 14:7-10, 19-22 or Joel 2:23-32   Psalm 84:1-7 or Psalm 65   2 Timothy 4:6-8, 16-18   Luke 18:9-14

Dates: October 23 – October 29

Reformation Sunday

Responsive Sentence for Reformation Sunday:
  We hear God's holy invitation: **"Be still and know that I am God."**

Heavenly Father, forgiver of our every sin, in Christ we are your new people. Your law is written on our minds and hearts. Your gospel is in the marrow of our bones. Our souls exalt with the good news of your new covenant with us. **R**

Lord God, our refuge and strength, your wondrous works make wars cease, plots fail, evil kingdoms totter. **R**

Lord Jesus Christ, through your work of atonement for us, the righteousness of God has been disclosed apart from the law. We dare not boast except in your loving and sacrificial death for our salvation. **R**

Holy Spirit, inspire us with the truth that makes us free from fear, free from eternal death, free to be your disciples of grace, love, joy, peace and patience. **R**

In the noise of our clamoring cities and factories, in the loud debates of opinion and politics, reform us by quieting all fears and doubts as we listen for you. **R**

Christ our King, weeping over Jerusalem, praying for us to Our Father, promising a crucified thief paradise, providing family beneath the cross for Mary your mother, and for John your disciple, we pray that you will care for us too. **R**

Hear our gratitude for hospitals, laboratories, institutions of learning; for nurses and doctors and family members who attend to our needs, and for churches like this gathering, where we boldly name the names of those who need your healing touch: _____. **R**

Reform us, make us your saints in this church militant, and in the life to come, make us your saints in the church triumphant. Be our one and only King.
Amen.

Texts: Jeremiah 31:31-34   Psalm 46   Romans 3:19-28   John 8:31-36

All Saints Sunday

Responsive Sentence for All Saints Sunday:
　　We hear God's holy invitation: **"Be still and know that I am God."**

Almighty God, Ancient One, even as you troubled Daniel's spirit because of his visions of you with the Messiah, give us the wisdom to seek the truth, and to ask your spiritual attendants for advice and comfort. **R**

Holy Spirit, as you take pleasure in our songs and praise, give us courage to sing, dance, and play music to the glory of God. **R**

Lord Jesus Christ, as we set our hopes and expectations on you, give us the heart of one who sees the future, and a spirit of wisdom and revelation as we come to know you better. **R**

Lord Jesus Christ, raised from the dead and seated at the right hand of God, you are the head of the church. We are your body, and you use us in ways we never quite understand or appreciate, for we know we are unworthy servants. **R**

Blessed and happy are we, Lord God, when we do unto others as we would have others do for us. As we study your teachings through the beatitudes, help us reverse our ways in every place you command. **R**

For all the saints, living on earth or in the hereafter, we rejoice in your power to heal, inspire and resurrect. Hear us as we name those whom you have placed in our lives to love, both in this world and the next: _____. **R**

Reform us, make us your saints in this church militant, and in the life to come, make us your saints in the church triumphant. Be our one and only King. **Amen.**

Texts:　Daniel 7:1-3, 15-18　Psalm 149　Ephesians 1:11-23　Luke 6:20-31

Time after Pentecost, Lectionary 31C

Responsive Sentence for the Sundays after Pentecost:
   Loving Christ: **Help us share the faith.**

Heavenly Father, you will not be bought off. You spurn offerings that do not require a change of heart, love of neighbor, or identification with the poorest of the poor. About this matter, Lord God, you are willing to argue. Yet you promise, that though our sins are like scarlet, you will make us as pure as new fallen snow, by the forgiving of our sins. **R**

Holy Spirit, we know that without you we are small and of little account. Give us the righteousness of Christ as a gift, that we may live joyfully with you and with one another and be true to your Word. **R**

Lord Jesus Christ, perfect our resolve and every work of faith we do out of love, knowing that your grace is far superior to all of our acts of kindness. **R**

Lord Jesus Christ, come, stay with us, like you did with curious Zacchaeus who climbed up a sycamore tree to see you. And when you come to stay with us, change us, just like every disciple was changed. **R**

Holy Spirit, we know that your inspiration isn't just for joy. You intend us to change the way we live and give. Be with us as we grow in the faith. **R**

We name names because you told us to pray for one another. Hear those in need of healing, rescue, encouragement or mercy: _____. **R**

Listening God, hear our prayers. **Amen.**

Texts: Isaiah 1:10-18 or Habakkuk 1:1-4, 2:1-4   Psalm 32:1-7 or Psalm 119:137-144   2 Thessalonians 1:1-4, 11-12   Luke 19:1-10

Dates: October 30 – November 5

Time after Pentecost, Lectionary 32C

Responsive Sentence for the Sundays after Pentecost:
   Loving Christ: **Help us share the faith.**

Heavenly Father, Job worried about his words and wished they were written in a book. Now they are. Even as he was first to announce the glorious news, "I know that my Redeemer lives," so fill us with your Holy Spirit that we may be so convinced. **R**

Holy Spirit, sometimes it is beyond us to imagine that we are the "apple of God's eye." Forgive us when we think we do not matter, since Our Redeemer says otherwise. **R**

Holy Spirit, we admit that the world and the church are often impatient and confused. We want action that no unbeliever can doubt. Purify our spirits, sanctify our lives, help us hold fast to the traditions of the faith. Thank you for giving us this, the very days and hours of our lives, that we may be gathered together with all of your saints. **R**

God of the living, even as you speak of Moses, Abraham, Isaac and Jacob in the present, you talk about all whom we have loved and lost for a while. To you, all are alive. God of the living, we trust in the resurrection of the dead. **R**

Holy Spirit, move over our land and touch the souls of those who dare to pray to you, believing that all three of our enemies: sin, death and the devil, are no monsters to you. They are but mere shadows, that have no eternal life. **R**

Jesus Christ, healer of our every ill, touch the hearts, bodies and souls of those whom we name before you: _____. **R**

Listening God, hear our prayers. **Amen.**

Texts: Job 19:23-27a or Haggai 1:15b—2:9   Psalm 17:1-9 or Psalm 145:1-5, 17-21 or Psalm 98
2 Thessalonians 2:1-5, 13-17   Luke 20:27-38

Dates: November 6 – November 12

YEAR C

Time after Pentecost, Lectionary 33C

Responsive Sentence for the Sundays after Pentecost:
    Loving Christ: **Help us share the faith.**

Heavenly Father, we revere your name as the God of our Lord and Savior Jesus Christ. On the last day, we anticipate His coming with the healing power of the resurrection. **R**

Holy Spirit, give us the vision of the day of reconciliation when the lamb and the wolf feed together, and the lion feasts on straw, like an ox. **R**

Lord Jesus Christ, when you return to this earth to resurrect the dead, may you find your servants serving, your people singing songs of praise, and our hearty welcome for the day of salvation. **R**

Holy Spirit, when the end of the world draws near and dreadful portents and great signs from heaven appear, fill us with boldness to testify to the new age dawning. **R**

Lord Jesus, first back from the dead with a body fit for eternal life, come when all is ready, that we may be where you are and celebrate the Great Reunion with all we have loved and lost. **R**

Lord Jesus, hear our heartfelt prayers as mortals for those among us who need healing: _____. **R**

Listening God, hear our prayers. **Amen.**

Texts: Malachi 4:1-2a or Isaiah 65:17-25   Psalm 98 or Isaiah 12   2 Thessalonians 3:6-13   Luke 21:5-19

Dates: November 13 – November 19

Christ the King, Lectionary 34C

Responsive Sentence for Christ the King:
    Rejoice to know: **Christ is King.**

Almighty God, when we shepherd your sheep wrongly, forgive us. Come, gather us together, and provide a shepherd worthy of serving you. **R**

Holy Spirit, still our anxious hearts and minds, for God is our refuge and strength, our help in the day of trouble. **R**

In the midst of a troubled world, Holy Spirit, counsel us to have no fear, for Christ the King is our Savior. **R**

Lord Jesus Christ, give us strength to endure all pains and sorrow, in the knowledge that by grace we have already been transferred into your kingdom. **R**

Jesus, Messiah, and King of kings, and Lord of lords, we know you will remember us on the day of resurrection. **R**

Holy Spirit, Counselor; Lord Jesus, King; Our Father, Lover; all we love are also loved by you. Hear us as we name those who need healing: _____. **R**

Reform us, make us your saints in this church militant, and in the life to come, make us your saints in the church triumphant. Be our one and only King. **Amen.**

Texts: Jeremiah 23:1-6   Psalm 46 or Luke 1:68-79   Colossians 1:11-20   Luke 23:33-43

Dates: November 20 – November 26

Made in the USA
Charleston, SC
22 December 2013